History of the Free Quakers

History

of the

Religious Society of Friends

called by some

The Free Quakers

in the

City of Philadelphia

Charles Wetherhill

Ross & Perry Inc.
Washington, D.C.

Printed in The United States of America

Ross & Perry, Inc. Publishers
216 G St., N.E.
Washington, D.C. 20002
Telephone (202) 675-8300
Facsimile (202) 675-8400
info@RossPerry.com

SAN 253-8555

Library of Congress Control Number:
http://www.rossperry.com.

ISBN 1-931839-19-0

Cover designed by Aakshi Sehdave. aakshi@rossperry.com
Book designed by Sapna Kartik. sapna@rossperry.com

⊗The paper used in this publication meets the requirements for permanence
established by the American National Standard for Information Sciences
"Permanence of Paper for Printed Library Materials" (ANSI Z39.48-1984).

PREFACE.

On the Southwest corner of Fifth and Arch Streets in the City of Philadelphia, there stands a small substantially built brick Meeting House, which has for many years been occupied by the Apprentices' Library Company. The gable end of the building fronts on Arch Street, and has built into it a marble tablet bearing this inscription :—

> " By General Subscription,
> For the Free Quakers, erected,
> In the year of our Lord, 1783,
> Of the Empire 8."

Nearly every building of the old City has, since this date, been torn down and replaced by edifices suited to the changing needs of commerce; but this house stands, the memorial of a past age, and is the only monument now left of the heroism of certain members of the Religious Society of Friends, in the stormy time of the Revolutionary War.

The story is now nearly forgotten, and if not recorded may perhaps soon be lost entirely, and it is for the purpose of preventing this; and to answer questions which the author of these notes has often been asked as to the origin of the Free Quakers, that he now attempts to revive from the torn and faded records of the old times, the history of that Society.

C. WETHERILL.

March 8, 1894.

I. Introductory—Colonial Period.

In considering the history of any Society, it is of the first importance to note its origin, and if it is a branch, or formed out of an older Society; then the antecedent history of the parent organization should be examined for that purpose.

As the Free Quakers were originally Orthodox Friends, their history will not be complete without some consideration of the nature of the Quakers and their peculiarities of faith and practice, for before the Revolutionary War the societies were identical. This is now briefly to be done, at the risk of repeating what has been better said before.

The organized followers of the religious teachings of George Fox called themselves "Friends," for they professed themselves to be friends, not merely of each other, but of all mankind. Their more common appellation of "Quakers" was applied to them in derision by their enemies.

Their belief was based upon this idea :—

They conceived it to be their duty strictly to follow the Divine commands, as contained in the Bible, according to their understanding thereof, and from this they made the further deduction that where God's command and human law seemed to them to be in conflict, they obeyed what seemed to them to be the Divine command, and willingly suffered the consequences, whatever they might be. They understood the Bible to contain an order to all men "to swear not at all," from which they inferred not only that

5

profane swearing was forbidden, but also that the oath taken by witnesses and jurors in judicial proceedings is equally immoral and wrong.

They read in Holy Writ that "all men are equal in the sight of God," and they therefore spoke of and addressed men of all ranks by name and not by title, and refused to show any mark of respect to any earthly magistrate.

They read the Divine command, "so far as possible to live at peace with all men," and interpreted this to mean a total prohibition of all war or strife, offensive or defensive, and they thereupon refused to serve in the army, or to make or trade in any munitions of war, or even to pay military taxes laid upon them, with their fellow subjects, by lawful authority.

They read that the Apostles "left all they had to follow the Lord," and were mostly poor and unlettered men, enlightened directly by the Spirit of God. They thereupon concluded to lead lives of extreme simplicity, and separate themselves from the vain follies of the world, and that the Gospel ought to be taught freely to all men, and that not by a priesthood supported by the government, or separated from the ordinary avocations of mankind, but by any person who felt impelled by the working of the Spirit within him to bear his testimony; also for this reason they refused to pay all tithes or taxes levied for the support of the lawfully established Church of England. Another consequence of their objection to a priesthood or ministry was, that, as there was no one to officially conduct or solemnize marriages among them, the marriage ceremony of the Quakers is a solemn contract signed and entered into by the parties themselves in the presence of witnesses, without the intervention of any priest or magistrate.

The result of the formation of a small sect earnestly
devoted to such doctrines, in the times of Charles the
Second, in England, might easily be foreseen by any one acquainted with the bigoted, yet dissolute, spirit of that period.

They were received wherever they appeared with derision
and scorn by the gay and polite courtiers, on account of
their simplicity of manners; with contempt by the soldiers,
by reason of their peaceful principles, and with stern disapprobation by the orderly and law-abiding, who viewed
with dismay their irregular conduct and doubtful marriages.
They were attacked alike by the corrupt, who found them an
easy prey on account of their principle of non-resistance,
and by the clergy, whose services they disturbed, and to
whom they refused to pay tithes. They were also punished by
the royal Government for their non-payment of taxes, their
failure to conform with the lawfully established religion, and
their refusal to serve in the army; and they received but
scant comfort in the courts of justice, where they steadfastly
refused to be sworn either as jurors or witnesses. The
elements of respectability and conservatism united with those
of disorder and corruption to punish and persecute them
with all possible rigor—and this they bore with the courage
and constancy of men filled with religious enthusiasm.

But when, after enduring these sufferings for a number of
years, William Penn was enabled to afford them the opportunity to emigrate to West Jersey and Pennsylvania, it was
thankfully accepted by many, and a colony largely composed
of Friends was speedily formed. Their most important
settlement at first was in Burlington, in West Jersey, where
the first yearly meeting was established on the third First day
of the Sixth month, 1681, but the superior advantages of
Philadelphia soon attracted to it a large number of settlers,

both Friends and others, and made it the chief town of the British colonies.

While many of the original colonists were not Friends, as, for instance, the Swedes, of Tinicum, and the German followers of Pastorius, in Germantown, yet the Friends were by far the most numerous and influential members of the new settlement. In their new and peaceful surroundings, the religious sentiments and belief of the Friends remained the same as before their emigration, yet some remarkable changes took place. Far removed from the tyranny of royal and priestly authority, and living in a country where there was no one to contend against them, they soon laid by the extravagant outbursts which had brought them into disrepute in England, and from being one of the most active and eccentric of all the religious sects, they soon became the most conservative and meditative, and the informality of their devotions soon by force of habit attained to a regularity almost ritualistic.

Their thrifty and industrious habits were soon rewarded by the accumulation of wealth, and although their plainness of speech and dress continued unchanged, prosperity engrafted upon their simple manners an aristocratic and dignified bearing, and the care of their large earnings gradually introduced among them a spirit of caution and conservatism.

They still, on principle, avoided the courts of justice, and each community or " Meeting " settled the disputes of their members by the arbitration of a Committee. The Committee in each Meeting soon assumed great power and authority, and under their leadership the private lives and concerns of their members were regulated in their most important and also in their most trivial details, with a strictness which in some particulars may have been necessary, but which was often exercised in a harsh and undiscriminating manner. For persisting in the use of wordly gayety of dress or household ornament, for marrying a person not a member of Meeting, for hasty violence of language, or striking any one, even in self-defence or in the defence of one's family, the same punishments of reprimand and disownment were decreed as if the offender were found guilty of the most disgraceful and immoral conduct, and from these sentences there was no practical appeal to any higher authority than those who pronounced them; for the appeal allowed to Quarterly and Yearly Meetings hardly availed the appellant, in Philadelphia, at least, where the Committee of the Monthly Meetings were also influential in the meetings to which the appeals were taken. While they were most benevolent in their works of charity to all men who needed help, whether they were Friends or not, there was but little kindness shown to Friends who disregarded the discipline laid down by the meeting.

Whatever feeling of discontent there may have been among members of the Religious Society of Friends in America at its rather severe discipline and occasional harsh enforcement, there was no open organized opposition to the system during the colonial period, but with the Revolution a more aggressive spirit arose. The war for freedom caused a great awakening of intellect in the American community; invaded by an overwhelming force, threatened with utter destruction, and thrown suddenly on their own resources, its sturdy, manly, Anglo-Saxon spirit rose nobly to the needs of the emergency. It not only produced the military genius of Washington and the soldiers who served with him, it warmed the eloquence of Henry and Adams, it enlivened the philosophy of Jefferson, it roused the varied talents for science and diplomacy of

Franklin, it strengthened alike the infidelity of Paine and the Christian devotion of Bishop White. It stirred the intellect and heart of the whole community to their very depths. And to relate the effect on the rich, peaceful, conservative Society of Friends is the object of this little history.

II. Revolutionary Period.

It is with no wish to cast reproach upon the respectable Society of Friends that the fact is recorded that at the commencement of the differences between the American colonists and the home Government, and until the event of war settled the points at issue in favor of the cause of freedom, the sympathies of those who controlled the public action of that society were with the Crown.

The leading members of that society were men who had grown old in the habit of loyalty, and had been rewarded therefor by dignities and wealth. Their government of the colony had always been peaceful; the spirit of resistance threatened war; and war was not only a subversion of their religious principles, but it threatened ruin to their worldly fortunes. With the habitual caution of men advanced in years, they looked with disfavor on the hot-headed young patriots who declared themselves supporters of so radical a change as the establishment of an independent government.

The calling together of the first Continental Congress was an act of heroic patriotism from the American standpoint, but was mere treasonable plotting in the royalists' eyes.

Accordingly, we find that at the General Yearly Meeting of Friends, held in Philadelphia in 1774, a letter was formally approved and ordered to be sent to all Meetings of Friends in America, warning all members of that Society not to depart from their peaceful principles by taking part in any of the political matters then being stirred up, reminding all Friends that under the King's government they had been favored with a peaceful and prosperous enjoyment of their rights, and strongly suggesting the propriety of disowning all such members as disobeyed the orders issued by the Yearly Meeting. This letter was generally respected and obeyed, and most Friends took no part in the war for freedom.

But this was not so with all: among the younger members many took an active part. These held that as they should render duty to their Government of willing obedience, so also they owed it their active support when threatened by invasion. While agreeing with their elders as to the wickedness of aggressive war and needless strife, they took the ground that it would be inconsistent to accept the support of the Continental Congress and armies, and refuse to aid them by every means possible. These men had to resist the prejudices which they had been educated in and by which they were surrounded. They had to meet their brethren before they went forth to meet the enemy; but they stood their ground without wavering. They served actively in the armies on the American side, they appeared in the Committee of Public Safety, they were seated in the Legislature, they were concerned in the printing of the Continental money. They gladly gave to the cause out of their purses and stocks of goods. Nor was it only by the men that these services were rendered, the women attended their husbands to the wars, and it is still remembered that during the battle of Trenton the wives of the Quaker soldiers helped on the battle-field to bandage the wounded, and the first flags that were carried by the American armies were made by a Quaker woman.

While this was being done, however, the Friends were not idle. They took prompt notice of the warlike propensities of their younger brethren, and the curious student of history who examines the records of Friends' meetings of that period will find a great number of entries like these:—

"*Isaac Howell* of this city who has made many years pro-
"fession of the Truth with us the people called Quakers, and
"we believe has been convinced of that divine principle
"which preserves the followers thereof from a disposition
"and conduct tending to promote war, has notwithstanding
"so far deviated therefrom as to manifest a disposition to con-
"tend for the asserting of civil rights in a manner contrary
"to our peaceable profession and principles, and accepted of
"and acted in a public station, the purpose and intention of
"which has tended to promote measures inconsistent there-
"with. It thereupon became our concern to treat with him,
"with desire to convince him of his error, but our labour of
"love not having the desired effect, and as the testimony of
"Truth has suffered by his means, and he doth not shew a
"disposition to condemn the same, We are under the
"necessity in order to support our Christian Testimony to
"declare that he hath separated himself from the Unity and
"fellowship of our Religious Society. Yet it is our earnest
"desire that he may become sensible of his deviations so as
"to manifest a just sense of his error, and by a due concern
"for the testimony of Truth, manifested by a suitable ac-
"knowledgement, become restored into membership."

Which entry means that Isaac Howell having disobeyed the precept of Yearly Meeting of 1774, and also having fallen away from correct following after Quakerism by accepting office under a government in rebellion, and by serving in a

military capacity, was thereupon disowned and excommunicated by the Philadelphia Meeting of Friends.

This action of Friends was not confined to the meetings in
Philadelphia; the following is a copy from the minutes of
the meeting at Wrightstown, in Bucks County:—

"From our Monthly Meeting of Friends, held at Wrights-
"town, the 4th day of the 11th month, 1777:—
:"Whereas, John Wilkinson hath had his birth and educa-
"tion amongst Friends, but hath so far disregarded the peace
"of society as to have served as a member of the Assembly,
"in the present unsettled state of affairs, contrary to the ad-
"vice of Friends; and, although repeatedly admonished on
"the occasion, doth not manifest a disposition to make the
"Meeting a proper acknowledgement for his outgoings:
"therefore, for the clearing of truth and our Society, we give
"forth this, our testimony, against such practices, and can
"have no further unity with him, the said John Wilkinson,
"as a member of our Society, until he come to a sense of his
"error, and condemn the same to the satisfaction of Friends,
"which that he may we desire for him. Signed in and on
"behalf of our said meeting by   J. CHAPMAN, *Clerk*."

The disowned members occasionally made vigorous protest
against the action of their Royalist brethren. The testimony
of the Wrightstown meeting against Thomas Ross, Jr., and
his testimony against the meeting which disowned him, are
an example of this, as the following copy will show:—

"From our Monthly Meeting held at Wrightstown, the
"7th of the 12th month, 1779:—
"Whereas, Thomas Ross, Jr., having had his birth and
"education amongst Friends, but having so far disregarded
"the testimony of truth against wars and fighting as to pay a
"fine demanded of him for not associating to learn the art of
"war; and Friends having treated with him in order to

" bring him to a sense of his misconduct, yet he continues to
" justify himself in so doing : therefore we give forth this as
" a testimony against such practices, and can have no further
" unity with him as a member of our Society, until he comes
" to a sense of his error and condemns the same to the satis-
" faction of Friends, which he may do is our desire for him.
" Signed in and on behalf of our said meeting by

" J. CHAPMAN, Clerk."

" When the clerk had finished reading the above testimony,
" Mr. Ross stood up and read the following declaration to
" the meeting :—

" Whereas, the Society of the people called Quakers, in
" North America, in several important particulars, both in
" theory and practice, have departed from their ancient
" creed, and inasmuch as, in their ecclesiastical decisions and
" transactions, they are become extremely partial, inconsist-
" ent, and hypocritical, I do therefore give forth this my tes-
" timony against their present practice and innovations, and
" can have no further unity with them as a member of their
" Society until they shall add to a profession more consistent
" with the doctrine of Christianity or practice more agreeable
" to their profession. Signed on behalf of himself by

" THOMAS ROSS, JR."

And this course was persisted in by the Quakers until near
the close of the Revolutionary War. Here is a certificate
dated in 1780 :—

" From our Monthly Meeting held at Buckingham, the 3d
" day of the 1st month, 1780 :—

" Joshua Ely, Jr., hath had his birth and education among
" the people called Quakers, and made profession with them ;
" yet he has been so unguarded, in this time of commotion
" and unsettled state of public affairs, as to take a test of alle-
" giance and abjuration ; and although he hath been labored
" with to convince him of the inconsistency thereof with our

"peaceable profession, so as to contemn him in so doing;
"but it has not had the desired effect, he endeavoring still to
"justify his conduct: therefore we do give forth this our tes-
"timony against him as a member in society with us until he
"comes to a sense of his error and makes satisfaction to the
"meeting, which he may is our desire for him. Signed by
"order and on behalf of our said meeting by
                "ROBERT KIRKBRIDE, *Clerk.*"

On June 13, 1777, the Legislature of Pennsylvania passed
a law commanding all residents to forthwith appear before
the justices or other officers qualified to administer judicial
oaths, and take oath or affirmation of allegiance to the State
of Pennsylvania and the United States, and abjure forever all
allegiance to the King and Government of Great Britain.
This brought the issue fairly and fully before the Society of
Friends; the leaders of that Society stood firm to the letter
of the Yearly Meeting of 1774, and generally failed to comply
with the law.   There can be no doubt that some, fearful alike
of disownment and of the punishment for treason on the
one hand, and of the penalties of the new law on the other,
took the oath of allegiance secretly, but some young Friends,
more earnest and candid than their brethren, attended publicly before the Justices and openly and willingly complied
with the law.   Among these was Samuel Wetherill, Junior,
who was a minister or public speaker at the meetings of
Friends, and also a very active man of affairs.   He was great-
grandson of Christopher Wetherill, one of the first settlers of
Burlington, in West Jersey, and one of the Council of Pro-
prietors which originally governed that colony.

Samuel was born in Burlington in 1736, and while a boy
came to Philadelphia and was apprenticed to Mordecai Yar-
nall, who was an eminent and pious preacher among the

Friends, and also a house carpenter. Like the good apprentice of Hogarth, he married his master's daughter, and by
attending diligently to business gained a good standing in
the city, and by his earnest and devout attention at meeting,
was much respected by the Friends. Just before the time
we now speak of, in 1775, he joined with Christopher Marshall and several other enterprising men in founding the first
factory for weaving cloth in the American Colonies, and
when the war broke out this factory was in active operation.
Not only did Samuel Wetherill publicly take the oath of
allegiance, but his public speech and ready pen were very
actively enlisted for the American cause.

The cloth woven by his factory was also supplied to the
army, and it is said that a timely shipment of these supplies
to the little army of Washington, at Valley Forge, saved it
from disbanding. He met his reward, the following entry
in Friends' Meeting Record attesting the same :—

"Whereas, *Samuel Wetherill* of this city hath many years
"made profession of the Truth with us, and we have grounds
"to hope he hath been convinced of the nature and excel-
"lency of Christian union and fellowship, but not being
"sufficiently attentive to the Divine principle of Gospel
"peace and love, which leads and preserves the followers of
"Christ out of contention and discord, has deviated from our
"ancient Testimony and peaceable principles, by manifest-
"ing himself a party in the public commotions prevailing,
"and taking a test of abjuration and allegiance, and hath also
"violated the established order of our Discipline by being
"concerned in publishing or distributing a book tending to
"promote dissension and division among Friends : It there-
"fore became our care to labour to convince him of the
"hurtful tendency of his conduct, but our brotherly concern
"and endeavours for him not being effectual, he persisting to
"vindicate his sentiments and proceedings in opposition to

"the united sense and judgment of Friends, we apprehend
"ourselves under the necessity, in support of our Christian,
"peaceable testimony, to declare that he hath separated
"himself from fellowship with us and become secluded from
"membership in our religious Society:—Nevertheless, we are
"sincerely concerned for his welfare and restoration, with
"desires that by his humble attention to the illumination of
"Divine Grace he may become so sensible of his deviation
"and errors as to be rightly restored into membership with
"us. 8th month, 1779."

What the book was that Samuel Wetherill published and
distributed is not now known: other literary works of his
that have survived to the present time, mostly on religious
subjects, are very forcibly expressed ; and upon those points
in which he differed from his brethren he probably expressed
himself with great clearness and vigor. Whatever their reply may have been, the only answer that has come down to
us is the above entry.

Not only in Philadelphia and its vicinity, but elsewhere in
the colonies, notably in Maryland and Massachusetts, many
Quakers were disowned for their service in the cause of their
country.

In considering the effects of disownment on those who
were thus disowned, it must be remembered that the Quakers
were, as they still are, an exceedingly religious people. Their
religion was not to them a mere external habit of devotion,
to be exhibited to other men on the First day of the week
and laid aside until the following First day. They meditated
on it daily ; it accompanied them in their round of duty and
business, the Bible was read and studied constantly, and
their meeting was far more to them than their place of
worship.

The Philadelphian of to-day has many places of amusement

2

and instruction which our ancestors of the Revolutionary time were without. In that little city, where the woods began at Fourth and Pine Streets, extending to the Schuylkill River, where the State House on Chestnut Street and the jail at Sixth and Walnut were almost out in the country, there were no theatres or concerts or lectures on subjects of popular interest, and no clubs or societies of a social kind, or at least very few. In that day the meeting was not only a place of religious worship, it was to Friends the chief place of social concourse as well, and he who was disowned for political cause was lonely indeed; for such a man was, in his heart, as truly a Quaker as any who disowned him. The services of the Established Church were as distasteful to him as they had been to Fox and Penn, so Christ Church had no attractions for him, and the bells of the little Swedish Lutheran Church of the Gloria Dei, ringing over the meadows of Moyamensing, called him in vain.

His heart yearned for the meeting, and its associations were none the less dear to him that he had been disowned, as it seemed to him, unjustly. As the Revolutionary War went on and the number of disowned Friends increased, they became something of a feature in the city, and the more devout among them began to meet together and compare views. It seems that they first met in small numbers in the autumn of 1780, at the houses of Samuel Wetherill and Timothy Matlack, and after a number of meetings for religious worship, the propriety of forming a meeting of their own was discussed among them. Several favored this action, and on the twentieth day of February, 1781, the new Society held its first meeting for business. The first minute book has been preserved, and it speaks of the Society as "The Religious Society of Friends, by some styled the Free Quakers."

A full list of the original members cannot be given, as some attended irregularly and failed to register their names,* but among the members the more conspicuous were the following :—

Timothy Matlack, who was a colonel in the army and a member of the Committee of Public Safety. Later he was a member of the State Legislature, and was a very active patriot.

White Matlack, brother of Timothy.

William Crispin, who was commissary in General Washington's Army.

Colonel Clement Biddle, a member of the well-known family of that name, who was disowned as early as 1775 for "studying to learn the art of war," he having raised a company of soldiers composed largely of Quakers. He afterward served as Quartermaster-General in the Revolutionary Army under General Gates, at Valley Forge and elsewhere.

Owen Biddle, his brother, who was a member of the State Legislature.

Benjamin Say, who was a well-known physician at that time.

Samuel Wetherill, Jr., who was the preacher and clerk of the meeting.

Christopher Marshall, who was a well-known patriot and an active member of the Committee of Public Safety. His diary has been published.

Joseph Warner, who served in the army and was at the Battle of Trenton.

Peter Thomson, who was employed by Congress to print the Continental money.

---

* *Vide* Appendix for a partial list of members.

Nathaniel Browne, Isaac Howell, Moses Bartram, and *Jonathan Scholfield* were also prominent members.

Among the women who were members the most famous were *Lydia Darragh* and *Elizabeth Griscom,* widow of John Ross, who afterward married John Claypoole. Lydia Darragh's house was used by certain British officers as their headquarters while their army occupied Philadelphia, and she accidentally overheard them plan a surprise, by night, of Washington's army, then encamped at White Marsh. She escaped from the city and conveyed news of the intended attack to the American army, and thus probably saved it and the American cause from destruction.

Elizabeth Claypoole lived in a small house on Arch Street, below Third, and was poor, supporting herself by her needle, and it is quite certain that the first American flags used in the army were made by her in June, 1776. The order of Congress directing her to be paid for this service has been preserved. The meeting of which she was a member disowned her for making the flags, and she, with her husband, who was a lieutenant in Colonel Eyre's regiment, joined the Free Quakers. She was of very gentle and amiable disposition, and it is gratifying to note that she lived to see the flag of her country, of which she made the oldest specimens, honored and respected all over the world. She was much loved by those who knew her, and was familiarly known as "Betsey" Claypoole. She outlived all the original members, dying at a very advanced age in 1836.

The Society was not a large one, the first meeting for business being attended by eight persons.

They and those who acted with them, feeling, no doubt, that in forming a new religious organization they ought to publicly make known their cause of so doing, prepared and

published an address to those of the people called Quakers
who have been disowned for matters religious or civil. This
was printed in what was then called "broadside" form, on a
single sheet of paper. It bears date "Philadelphia, 24th of
the 4th month, 1781," and a copy will be found in the
Appendix. This, the first public, printed utterance of the
Society, should be carefully studied, and when it is remembered that at this time the American cause seemed almost
hopeless, the Congress without money or credit, and our
armies defeated and discouraged, the patriotic language of
this and the other early documents of the Society is worthy
of particular note. It calls upon those who have been disowned and feel the need of religious worship to join with
them in discharging their religious duties to themselves and
their children and families, and reminding the disowned that
many of them have been turned away from the Society in
which they were educated "for no other cause than a faithful
"discharge of those duties which we owe to our country;" it
assures them that "we have no new doctrine to teach, nor
"any design of promoting schisms in religion," . . . . but
"mean to pay a due regard to the principles of our fore-
"fathers. We have no desire to form creeds or confessions
"of faith, but humbly to confide in those sacred lessons of wis-
"dom and benevolence which have been left to us by Christ
"and His apostles contained in the Holy Scriptures, and
"appealing to that divine principle, breathed by the breath of
"God into the hearts of all, to leave every man to 'think and
"judge for himself, according to the abilities received, and to
"answer for his faith and opinions to Him who 'seeth the
"secrets of all hearts,' the Sole Judge and Sovereign Lord of
"Conscience." The faith of the new meeting, therefore, was
the Quaker faith in which they had been brought up. The same

simplicity of life, the same Christian belief, the same trust in the Bible as the Word of God, the same appeal to "a divine "principle directly sent from God into the hearts of all men," which has been the constant claim of the teachers of that faith from the beginning, was asserted fully and emphatically in this characteristic address. The differences indicated were not of faith, but of practice; but they were so original as to be very remarkable. The Free Quakers were fighting for the same liberty in matters of religion that they had contended for, and were in the act of winning politically. They had faced the power of England, they were in the act of establishing a republican government for America. They also wished to form a Church in which its members would be as free from the tyranny of bishops and ruling elders as they sought to be free from the despotic rule of a foreign and distant King. The first point with them was that in the new meeting no man who believed in God, in a supreme, wise, and benevolent Ruler of the Universe, and who joined with them, should be disowned or excommunicated for any cause whatever. It was charged against them that under such lax discipline dangerous new doctrines might be preached. It was answered, "better to suffer the dangers of freedom than the coldness of repression," and if any is clearly wrong, better to advise with him kindly than to turn him away. It was charged that such a discipline left it in the power of one member to pronounce opinions at variance with those of all the rest of the meeting. It was answered that such a single member might be in the right and his brethren in error. It was charged that the new Society might be disgraced by the possible immoral conduct of its members if such were not disowned. It was answered that the Church is a moral and spiritual hospital, wherein measures ought to be taken to heal the diseased, and that the more sinful a member seemed to be, the more evident is the necessity of laboring for his reformation, and that if any supposed disgrace attended on companionship with offenders, that inconvenience was more than repaid if they could be thereby brought to reform and sin no more.

On one other point they differed radically from the older Society, and that was as to the right of offering forcible resistance against warlike invasion. The Quakers had always held that resistance was sinful, and so they adhered to an absolute peace, under all circumstances, suffering violence to themselves, their families, and their country rather than offer any resistance or serve in the army, even going so far as to refuse to pay taxes where the money was being raised for military purposes. The Free Quakers held, admitting the necessity of government, that all government is essentially a defensive war for the protection of public peace, and that when the government is threatened by domestic treason or foreign invasion; it then becomes the plain duty of every man to join in the public defence by all means possible, and that war, while an extreme measure, is in such instances not merely justifiable, but right and proper, and, as is shown above, the founders of the Society showed their sincerity in this matter by serving their country, with their very best exertions, at the time of its utmost need. On the same ground they held, contrary to the discipline of Friends, that a man might forcibly resist any bodily violence offered to himself or to any one to whom he owed the duty of protection. While their views as to warfare and resistance were precisely the same as that of nearly all Christians, they were in such striking contrast to the well-settled doctrines of the Friends that they were commonly known, and are still sometimes spoken of, as "*Fighting*" Quakers.

These views they very firmly adhered to and very forcibly
set forth at their meetings for worship by the preaching of
Samuel Wetherill, who about this time or probably a little
later—for the work bears no date—wrote and published a
small pamphlet entitled "An Apology for the Religious
"Society called Free Quakers in the City of Philadelphia,"
in which he argues very strongly that all Churches who
excommunicate act inconsistently with the Gospel, and in
which he also states with great strength and clearness the
views of the Society on the doctrine of non-resistance. The
book is very interesting, as showing clearly in what points
they differed from their Orthodox brethren.

Among other things he says (pp. 34, 35) :—

"Those who believe the Society of Friends are the
"Church of Christ, and that disowning necessarily implies
"an exclusion from Heaven, are, according to the ancient
"principle laid down by Barclay, the true and orthodox
"Quakers. The others who do not suppose the Society are
"the pure Church, who do not pretend to binding and
"loosing in heaven and on earth, are most catholic and
"modest. But let me ask those friends : supposing a num-
"ber of men were forming themselves into a religious society
"for the purposes of improvement in piety and virtue, would
"the present discipline of Friends be the most proper rules
"to produce this effect? Would they agree that no one
"among them should marry a person of any other Society,
"though ever so amiable, under pain of being expelled from
"the body, nor even a member of their own Society, unless
"they accomplished their marriage agreeable to one par-
"ticular form? That no man should defend his own life,
"nor the life of his friend, nor the government under which
"he lived, nor pay taxes for military purposes, nor a fine for

"not complying with the laws in certain cases? That no
" man should publish a religious or political treatise without
" consent of the Society, under the penalty of being expelled
" from the body? Can it be supposed that any number of
" men of sound understanding would, in the present day,
" lay down such a plan, and make a compliance with those
" rules the test of Christian fellowship? If, then, it is
" impossible to suppose such a case, are they wise who make
" those rules the test of Christian fellowship, merely because
" they were made the conditions of fellowship by their ances-
" tors? How much more reasonable would it be in them
" to say: the design of this institution is, that we may be
" mutually instrumental in promoting the temporal and eter-
" nal felicity one of another? We feel the importance of a
" virtuous life, we will, therefore, use all the means with
" which divine providence may favour us, solely for this end.
" If, then, a brother should be overtaken in a fault, we will
" endeavour to restore such a one in the spirit of meekness,
" considering ourselves, lest we also be tempted; but in no
" case whatever, shall any one be expelled from the Society,
" lest it should prove his ruin. How greatly preferable
" would such a system of church government be? * * *
" Such, then, is the plan of the Religious Society of Free
" Quakers in the City of Philadelphia."

Their meetings for worship were at first held in private
houses, generally in the house of the clerk. Afterwards, they
met in one of the rooms of the college building of the Uni-
versity of Pennsylvania.

At their meetings for business, their first work was to for-
mulate a Discipline, or plan of organization, and in order to
obtain the assistance of all such disowned Friends as might
wish to join in the work, they issued on the fourth day of

the sixth month, 1781, a second broadside or public printed
letter to "Our Friends and Brethren in Pennsylvania, New
Jersey and elsewhere," stating that they "conceived it to
"be a duty which we owe to ourselves, our children, and
"families to establish and support among us public meetings
"for religious worship, and to appoint stated meetings for
"conducting the affairs of the Society, upon principles as
"liberal and enlarged toward one another, as those adopted
"by the State are toward all," and inviting "the advice and
"assistance of all who may kindly afford us their counsel."
This letter will also be found copied at length in the
Appendix. Having sent out this epistle to their friends,
they continued their work on Discipline, and on the sixth
day of the eighth month, 1781, at their meeting for business,
unanimously agreed to it. The document has been printed,
and a clearer or more forcibly expressed work of the kind
could hardly be imagined. It is so filled with a manly spirit
of patriotism, mingled with Christian devotion, and also
showing a due sense of order which has always characterized
the Friends, that this work would not be complete unless it
be transcribed in full.

This, then, is

"THE DISCIPLINE.

OF THE

Society of Friends, by some styled the Free Quakers.

*Unanimously agreed to in their Meeting for Business, held in Philadel-
phia on the Sixth day of the Eighth Month, 1781.*

"The Creator of man, having bestowed upon individuals
"greater and less natural abilities, and opportunities of im-
"provement, a variety of sentiments respecting the duties

"which we owe to him, necessarily arises among us, and it
"becomes essential to our happiness, that we may perform
"those duties in that way which we think most acceptable to
"him. And therefore, when we contemplate the long con-
"tinued and earnest contest which has been maintained, and
"the torrents of blood which, in other countries, have been
"shed in defence of this precious privilege, we cannot but
"acknowledge it to be a signal instance of the immediate care
"of a divine providence over the people of America, that he
"has, in the present great revolution, thus far established
"among us governments, under which no man, who acknowl-
"edges the being of a God, can be abridged of any civil
"right on account of his religious sentiments; while other
"nations who see and lament their wretched situation are yet
"groaning under a grievous bondage. But governments
"established upon those liberal, just, and truly christian prin-
"ciples, and wisely confined to the great objects of ascer-
"taining and defending civil rights, in avoiding the possi-
"bility of wounding the conscience of any, must unavoidably
"leave some cases unprovided for, which come properly
"under the care of religious societies. Hence we are not
"only left at liberty to act agreeably to our sentiments; but
"the necessity and obligation of establishing and supporting
"religious societies are increased and strengthened.

"We acknowledge the kindness of providence in awaken-
"ing us to a view of the deplorable situation in which we
"have been. Disowned and rejected by those among whom
"we have been educated, and scattered abroad, as if we had
"been aliens in a strange land, the prospect of our situation
"has indeed humbled us. But he whose mercy endureth
"forever has preserved us, and induced us to confide that he
"will care for us. And being made sensible of the indispen-

"sable necessity of uniting together, we have cast our care
"upon the great preserver of men, and depending upon him
"for our support, conceive it to be a duty which we owe to
"ourselves, our children, and families, to establish and sup-
"port among us public meetings for religious worship; to
"appoint stated meetings for conducting the affairs of the
"Society, upon principles as liberal and enlarged toward one
"another, as those adopted by the state are toward all, and
"paying a due regard to the principles of our forefathers,
"and the spirit of the wise regulations established by them,
"to fix upon such rules as may enable us to preserve decency
"and good order; and among other things, to agree upon,
"and make known a decent form of marriage, which may at
"once secure the rights of parents and of children; and a
"mode of forming and preserving records of marriages,
"births, and burials.

"Wherefore after mature deliberation it was unanimously
"agreed as follows, to wit :—

"*First.*—Meetings for public worship shall be established
"and kept up. The time and place of holding them shall
"be ordered and directed by the meeting for business. And
"it is earnestly recommended, to all who come to our meet-
"ings for worship, or meetings for business, to attend pre-
"cisely at the time appointed.

"*Secondly.*—A meeting shall be held monthly for conduct-
"ing the business of the Society, in which any member may
"freely express his sentiments, on all business which shall
"there be determined or considered. In this meeting una-
"nimity and harmony ought to prevail, and where any differ-
"ence of sentiment may appear, charity and brotherly con-
"descension ought to be shown to one another. Minutes of
"all the proceedings shall be kept, and for this purpose a

" clerk shall be appointed, and be under the direction of the
" meeting. At the opening of each meeting, after a solemn
" pause for worship, the minutes of the meeting next pre-
" ceding shall be read.

" *Thirdly*.—Persons intending marriage may, either in
" person or by a friend, inform the meeting for business there-
" of; but where it may conveniently be, it is recommended,
" that the parties proposing marriage do attend the meeting
" before which the proposal is made. Whereupon a com-
" mittee shall be appointed to enquire concerning their clear-
" ness of other marriage engagements, consent of parents or
" guardians; and such other matters as relate to the proposed
" marriage, and report thereon to the next meeting. No
" reasonable objection appearing, and the parties as afore-
" said signifying the continuation of their intentions, the
" marriage may be allowed of, and two persons appointed to
" attend the decent solemnization thereof, and to have the
" certificate of the same recorded in the book of marriages.

" The marriage may be solemnized at a public meeting for
" worship; or at the house of either of the parties; or at the
" house of their parents or friends, as the parties may choose:
" but it is recommended that the same be preceded by a
" solemn pause, and worship to God. As cases may probably
" happen, in which it will be inconvenient to postpone mar-
" riages so long as from one monthly meeting to another, in
" such cases an adjournment of the meeting may be made,
" the report of the committee received, and the marriage be
" allowed of as aforesaid.

" The solemnization is recommended to be after the fol-
" lowing manner, to wit: The parties standing up and taking
" each other by the hand, the man shall declare to this import:
" That he takes the woman, naming her name, to be his wife,

"and will be unto her a loving and faithful husband until
"death shall separate them. And the woman, on her part,
"shall declare to the import That she takes the man, naming
"his name, to be her husband: and will be unto him a loving
"and faithful wife until death shall separate them. The cer-
"tificate whereof may be to the following import, to wit:
"Whereas, A. B., of C., (expressing also his title or occupa-
"tion,) son of C. D., of E. and F. his wife, and G. H.,
"daughter of I. K., of L., and M., his wife, having laid
"their intentions of marriage with each other, before the
"meeting for business of the society of Friends, styled by
"some The Free Quakers, held at N., the same were allowed
"of, and on the   day of the   month, in the year
"of our Lord (inserting the day, month, and year), the said
"parties appeared at a meeting appointed for the solemniza-
"tion of the said marriage (or otherwise as the case may be),
"and taking each other by the hand, the said A. B., did, in
"a solemn manner, declare that he took the said G. H., to
"be his wife, and promised to be unto her a loving and
"faithful husband until death should separate them: And the
"said G. H., did in like manner declare, that she took the
"said A. B. to be her husband, and promised to be unto
"him a loving and faithful wife until death should separate
"them. And in confirmation and testimony of the same,
"they the said A. B. and G. H., she assuming the name of
"her husband, did then and there to these presents set
"their hands. And we, whose names are also subscribed,
"being present at the said marriage and subscription, have,
"as witnesses to the same, hereunto set our hands, the day
"and year aforesaid.

"*Fourthly.*—Records shall be kept of all marriages, births,
"and burials among us. And as these records may be of

"great importance, and the recording of births and burials
"will greatly depend on the care of individuals, in giving an
"account thereof, it is earnestly recommended to all, to give
"an early account of both, mentioning the child's name,
"parentage, and day of its birth; and the name, parentage,
"title or occupation, age, and day of decease, as well of
"those who die abroad, when the same can be ascertained,
"as of those who die among us.

"*Fifthly.*—Persons desirous of joining with us in Society,
"signifying the same to the meeting for business, and appear-
"ing to be of good character, may be admitted. Whereupon
"they may give in the names and ages of their children, to
"be recorded. Should any choose to go from among us, a
"minute thereof may be entered among our proceedings.

"*Sixthly.*—In cases of controversy respecting property, a
"reference to disinterested men, either of our own or some
"other Society, and a compliance with their judgment, may
"be recommended, as the most expeditious and least expen-
"sive mode of terminating such disputes, and tending to
"peace and harmony, but, it shall be a perpetual rule among
"us, as a religious society, that we will not otherwise inter-
"fere in controversies between one man and another. This
"rule being contrary to that of our ancestors, in this case we
"think it necessary to observe, That however blameable or
"even "shameful" it might have been in the Apostle's day,
"for brother to go to law with brother "before the un-
"believers," in the present day, when the State, of which
"we ourselves are members, appoint men eminent for their
"abilities and integrity, to judge of all controversies, and
"those judges being themselves Christians, are aided by juries
"of Christians: there does not appear any just cause for pro-
"hibiting appeals to them: on the contrary, to us it seems

"to be indecent and unjust to speak of these Christian courts,
"as the Apostles spake of those of "the unbelievers," and as
"the Society who have disowned us have affected to speak
"of the courts of justice, even when themselves were the
"officers, jurors, judges, and legislators.

"*Seventh.*—As brethren each may counsel and advise an-
"other in the spirit of love and meekness, as he may see
"occasion, remembering always that he also may be tempted:
"but leaving guilt to be punished by the laws of the land, and
"commending those who err to the grace of God, no public
"censures shall be passed by us on any. Neither shall a
"member be deprived of his right among us, on account of
"his differing in sentiment from any or all of his brethren."

This paper is as remarkable in its utterances as in its
omissions. One searches through it in vain for any creed
or protestation of faith; and the Discipline would be almost
as suitable, in its simple arrangements, for a society of ancient
Greek philosophers. The society was from its origin de-
voutly and earnestly Christian, but they were Quakers, and
their disownment having been only for civil or political
cause, and not on any ground of religious difference, their
belief on all main points was already so clearly understood
that no publication of it was deemed needful or advisable.

The Discipline however points clearly to the main grounds
wherein they differed from Friends. The closing statement
"Neither shall a member be deprived of his right among
"us on account of his differing in sentiment from any or
"all of his brethren," is an assurance of religious freedom
which no other Christian sect has ever given to its followers.

These publications attracted considerable attention at the
time, especially among Friends, and members of that Society in other States who had suffered disownment began

to organize and meet in the same manner. In Chester County in Pennsylvania, at West River in Maryland, even as far as Massachusetts, Free Quaker meetings began to spring up, and a regular correspondence between these Friends and the Philadelphia meeting seems to have existed.

Meanwhile the Society in Philadelphia was much inconvenienced for want of some suitable place in which to hold their meetings for worship and business. Application was made to the Friends who had disowned them for leave to use one of the meeting houses of that Society, but this was refused. The Free Quakers consulted thereon, and, holding that their expulsion had been mainly caused by political differences, with which a religious sect as such had nothing to do, and as they had been disowned for simply obeying the laws and devoting their lives and property to the service of their country, they conceived that their disownment for such causes gave their orthodox brethren no right to exclude them from the joint use of the meeting houses and burial ground of the Quakers. In this view many persons who were not of that Society agreed with them, for the Whig Quakers, or Fighting Quakers, as they were called, had the sympathies of the people with them. Thus cheered, they prepared a formal printed letter, "From the Monthly Meeting of Friends, called by some the Free Quakers, held by adjournment at Philadelphia, on the ninth day of the seventh month, 1781: To those of our Brethren who have disowned us," which states the differences that had arisen and proceeds: "We think it proper for us to use, apart from you, "one of the houses built by Friends in this city for those "purposes;" * * * * "and therefore we thus invite "you to the opportunity of showing what degree of kindness "and brotherly love toward us still remains among you.

"We also mean to use the burial ground whenever the occa-
"sion shall require it; for, however the living may contend,
"surely the dead may lie peaceably together."

The original letter was presented by Timothy Matlack,
Moses Bartram, and White Matlack, to the Monthly Meeting
of Friends in Philadelphia, on the twenty-seventh day of
seventh month, 1781. On the back of the letter is a memorandum, evidently made by some member of the Meeting
to whom it was delivered, of the proceedings of the Quakers
thereupon and the verbal answer which it was agreed should be
made to Timothy Matlack or "either of the persons who
attended with him," and which was done accordingly.
Probably by some mistake, the original letter was returned,
together with the endorsed memorandum, so we know just
what the verbal answer was. It ran as follows :—

"We have considered the contents of the paper presented
"to our last meeting by Timothy Matlack and others, and
"are of the judgment that it is improper to be read in the
"Meeting, of which we think the parties concerned will
"have grounds to be convinced, on a cool and dispassionate
"reconsideration, of the requisition they make." [For a
full copy see Appendix, No. 3.]

This answer amounting to a final refusal, the Free Quakers
applied to the Legislature of the State, alleging their right
and stating that they and others had been disowned by the
leading men of that Society on various pretences, among
them the following :—

"Some have been disowned for affirming allegiance to
"the State in compliance with the laws, and their elders
"and overseers have proposed and insisted on a renun-
"ciation of that allegiance as a condition of reunion with
"them.

"Some for holding office under the State, and some for "holding office under the United States.

"Many for bearing arms in defence of our invaded "country, although the laws of the State enjoined and "required it of them.

"And some have been disowned for having paid the taxes "required of them by law;" and they closed by praying for leave to bring in a bill for recognizing the rights of persons disowned by the people called Quakers, to hold in common with them the estates owned by them, and the right to search and copy their records. This petition virtually charged the managers of the Quaker Society with acting in complicity with the royalists and treasonably against the American government. This petition was signed by about fifty men, and was presented to the Legislature on the twenty-first of December, 1781. [A copy will be found in the Appendix, No. 4.]

This petition was answered by an address and memorial on behalf of the people called Quakers, signed the eighteenth of First Month, 1782, by John Drinker, clerk of their meeting, and which was probably presented to the Legislature at about the time of its date. This denies any treasonable intent by the Quakers, and sets forth that in disowning the members as charged they had simply acted upon the rules of their Society and well established discipline, and that in so doing they had only exercised that degree of religious freedom which was guaranteed to all bodies of Christians by the law, and that in refusing to join in warlike measures in support of political freedom, they were only obeying their consciences and the Divine Command, according to their understanding.

And so the Commonwealth in its first days was presented with the question: How far is the exercise of freedom in matters of religion to be considered an excuse for non-compliance with the laws of the land.

On the one hand it was urged that the liberty of every man to worship God, and in matters of religion to act according to the dictates of his conscience, was solemnly guaranteed by law, from the time of the settlement of the colony by William Penn. On the other hand it was argued with equal earnestness, that where the State is in danger she has a right to call upon all her citizens for support, and to punish any who make their conscientious scruples an excuse for disobedience. The question was not only debated in the Legislature, but also with considerable earnestness in the public press; several broadsides and small pamphlets were published at about this time on the subject. The several memorials to the legislature were very able statements, from the supporters of each side of the controversy, though it is rather sad to note, that the affectation of a Christian meekness in their language, really covered great bitterness of spirit on both sides. The legislature very wisely refused to decide the question, or place any written limits either to the right of the government to demand support, or of tender consciences to have special respect and favor. And the question has not been decided to the present time, but remains open; so that each case may be decided on the merit of its particular facts. As to the petition of the Free Quakers, it was tabled, and nothing further was done during that session of the legislature. The matter was revived however, at the next session, by a memorial and remonstrance presented by Isaac Howell and White Matlack, which set out their claims and those of the other Friends disowned on political grounds, at length, and repeated the prayer of the petition which had been presented before. This address was presented in the House of Representatives on August 21, 1782, entered on the journal at length and referred to a special committee. To the public interest caused by this address we are indebted, as one result was that the answer of the Quakers to the original petition was published and a printed copy has been preserved. It, together with the remonstrance of Howell and Matlack, will be found in the Appendix. The committee, however, took no action and the legislature did nothing in the matter. Isaac Howell presented a short petition, asking the consideration of the House to the subject, early in 1783, and this was accompanied by a letter signed by thirty-seven of the disowned Quakers, joining in the request of the petition, but the legislature adjourned without taking any action.

Meanwhile, however, Cornwallis had surrendered to General Washington, the English forces had abandoned New York, the revolutionary war had come to an end by virtue of the treaty with England which acknowledged the independence of the American Colonies, and the State of Pennsylvania became a sovereign power. The Whigs having thus won their cause, felt a strong sympathy with those of the Quakers who had suffered disownment by the religious society in which they were born, for the sake of their attachment to the new republic just being established. Prominent citizens felt and said that the disowned Friends had been hardly and unjustly dealt with. The Free Quakers began to raise money and take steps to build a meeting house for themselves, and Samuel Wetherill, White Matlack, Jehu Eldridge and Isaac Howell, were on June 16, 1783, appointed a committee to find a suitable lot of ground on which to build. And on the seventh day of July, 1783, Samuel Wetherill on behalf of the committee, reported to a meeting for business that he had obtained a lot suitable for the purpose at the southwest corner

of Fifth and Mulberry, or Arch Streets, in front on Mulberry
Street forty-eight feet, in depth on Fifth Street sixty feet,
which he held ready to convey to trustees. The Society of
Free Quakers, thereupon approved the action of their committee, and appointed a Board of Trustees to accept from
Samuel Wetherill a conveyance of the lot. The following
were the Trustees:—

CHRISTOPHER MARSHALL, SR., Gentleman,
NATHANIEL BROWNE, Blacksmith,
ISAAC HOWELL, Esquire,
PETER THOMSON, Conveyancer,
MOSES BARTRAM, Druggist,
JONATHAN SCHOLFIELD, Shop-keeper,
BENJAMIN SAY, Practitioner in Physic,
JOSEPH WARNER, Last Maker, and
ABRAHAM ROBERTS, Grocer.

And on the tenth day of the same month, a deed of the lot
was duly executed to them accordingly, in trust "to and for
"the use and benefit of the Religious Society of People,
"distinguished and known by the name of Free Quakers, in
"the City of Philadelphia, to erect and build a meeting house
"thereon, and therein to meet, for the solemn worship of
"Almighty God, the Creator, Upholder, and Ruler of the
"Universe." And they at once and unanimously resolved
to build a meeting house thereon, and forward a subscription
to defray the expense of so doing, and "a disposition to aid
us appearing to be general," as the minutes state, at the next
meeting they somewhat enlarged the plan of their building, and
appointed White Matlack treasurer, directing him to "keep all
money received and to be received by him in the bank."
The Bank of North America, then newly established, which
was incorporated, May 26, 1781, and began active business
January 7, 1782, is undoubtedly referred to, for the Pennsyl-

vania Bank, which had been founded in 1780 to make the necessary arrangements to supply the American army with the munitions of war, was never a bank of general deposit, and was at this time preparing to wind up its affairs, and these two were then the only banks in the United States, and Timothy Matlack was a director of the Bank of North America at its formation.

The subscription prospered; among the contributors to the building fund were Washington, Franklin, and a number of other distinguished patriots, and the Meeting House was built accordingly. When the wall was nearly finished, and the marble tablet was about being built into its place, one of the Free Quakers was asked why the words "in the year of the "Empire 8" were inserted. He answered, "I tell thee, "Friend, it is because our country is destined to be the great "empire over all this world."

One little circumstance illustrating the customs that then prevailed may perhaps be mentioned. The religious people of that day had not yet taken the earnest stand in regard to the use of alcoholic drink which has since distinguished the Society of Friends; the query was still asked at their yearly and other meetings, "Whether Friends were careful to keep "their laborers in harvest and elsewhere duly supplied with "spirits," and the Free Quakers, on this subject at least, agreed with their orthodox brethren. When the roof of the Meeting House was completed, in 1784, refreshment was provided to the laborers, and the receipted bill for the rum, lemons and sugar, with which they were entertained, is preserved to this day among the papers of the Society.

The Meeting House was completed early in 1784, and worship was first held in it on the thirteenth of June in that year, and regularly thereafter on every Sunday for many years.

The notes of the meetings for business continue during this period to show considerable correspondence with the disowned Friends of Massachusetts, several of whom visited the Society in Philadelphia, and Samuel Wetherill at about this time went on a religious visit to these Friends and was absent for several months. It seems that meetings on similar principles to the Society in Philadelphia were organized at Long Plain, near Dartmouth, at Rochester, and elsewhere.

The Society, though now prospering, was without any graveyard; but in 1786 a law was passed, vesting certain city lots in trustees for a burial ground for the use of the Society. This act was passed August 26, 1786, and recites that it is but right and just to forward the "designs of religion and "benevolence, and that the virtuous citizens of this common- "wealth who have been deprived of their religious rights and "privileges on account of their attachment to the cause of "their country in the time of its utmost danger, should have "the encouragement of the Legislature," and proceeds to grant public city lots Nos. 34 to 41, on west side of Fifth Street below Locust Street, to "Christopher Marshall, Joseph "Stiles, Nathaniel Browne, Isaac Howell, Peter Thomson, "Benjamin Say, and Joseph Warner, and the survivors and "survivor of them, and the heirs and assigns of such survivor "forever: In trust, nevertheless, to and for the sole purpose "of a burial ground for the use of the Religious Society of "Friends distinguished and known by the name of Free "Quakers, in the City of Philadelphia."

Being now established with all the property and rights usual to religious societies, the Free Quakers entered upon a prosperous career. Their meetings for worship were well attended; the upper room of their meeting house was rented at first to the Masonic Lodge of which Washington was a member, and afterwards to one Benjamin Tucker, who kept a school there, and the rents thus obtained were formed into a fund for the charitable relief of the poor members of the Society. And the history of the meeting soon became, as shown by the minutes, almost as peaceful and uneventful as that of the Orthodox Friends who had disowned them. Meanwhile, the political differences which had caused their separation from the Orthodox Friends were fast disappearing.

After 1783 the query, "Are Friends careful not to defraud the King of his dues?" was not asked in their yearly and other meetings, and they gladly joined with their more enterprising fellow citizens in obedience to the republican form of government, and in 1789 their yearly meeting sent a letter to Washington on the occasion of his inauguration as President, congratulating him, and wishing long life and prosperity both to him and his "amiable consort." Washington replied in courteous terms to this address, which marks the complete and loyal recognition by the Quakers of the American government, which that people have always since maintained. And while they did not formally amend their discipline, in the matter of disownment, they, and indeed all bodies of Christians, have since become so liberal and merciful to the shortcomings of individual members, that it may almost be said that the doctrines of Free Quakers on this point are now generally accepted everywhere. The Friends, however, could not bring themselves into harmony with the Free Quakers, and in 1790 sent word to Samuel Wetherill forbidding him to speak in their grave-yard, to which he replied in a letter to their ministers' meeting, stating his intention at all proper times and places to bear his testimony in the cause of virtue and truth, of which a copy will be found in the Appendix. It seems also that he was spoken of as an infidel, to which charges he replied by writing a pamphlet entitled, "The Divinity of Jesus Christ Proved."

As the political differences died away, some of the revolutionary soldiers made acknowledgment to their meetings and were received back into membership with Friends, and so before long the Free Quakers, never a very large body, became comparatively few in number; held together principally by the talent and exertions of their clerk and preacher, Samuel Wetherill; he served the society as clerk until September 1st, 1808, when he resigned and was succeeded by his son of the same name, and he continued active in the ministry until his death, in his eighty-first year, in 1816. Before his death the disowned Friends of Maryland, Massachusetts, and Ohio, had all died, or been taken back into their meetings, and the Free Quakers were a small and rapidly diminishing band of the revolutionary heroes of Philadelphia. Religious worship was faithfully observed by them every Sunday. Clement Biddle died in 1813. Samuel Wetherill, Jr., died in 1829. Timothy Matlack, removed from the city, and died in 1829, at Holmesburg, in the 100th year of his age. Elizabeth Claypoole, the last survivor of the original members, died in 1836. The families of the first members ceased to attend Sunday meetings, and John Price Wetherill, who succeeded his father as clerk, after worshipping nearly alone for several years, closed the meeting for the last time, and meetings for religious worship ceased about 1836.

III. The Modern Period.

When the meetings for worship of the Free Quaker Society came to an end, the Society would almost certainly soon have been disbanded and become extinct, like the similar societies in other parts of the country, had it not been for the wisdom and energy of the clerk, John Price Wetherill.

He recognized that a religious sense of devotion may be as well expressed in an honest life and in charitable works as by formally attending church or meeting at fixed intervals of time, and that, as by the growth of the city and the removal of the members to a distance, it became inconvenient to attend religious meetings, they ought still in some organized and distinct form to work as a charity, thereby recognizing that charity conducted on a proper motive is religion and worship, which Friends have always believed. Almost immediately upon his becoming clerk, in 1829, he perfected the organization of a charitable committee in the Society, to use its income in some way for the benefit of the poor, first of the Society, and then for the poor generally, and when the cessation of formal meetings for religious worship left the Society in possession of a vacant building, his practical disposition soon turned it to good account. Several years before, a number of public-spirited citizens had joined in forming a library, primarily for the use of the apprentices and young persons employed in the city, but also for the use of any orderly person who might wish to study. This was then, and for many years continued to be, the only free library in the city, and the amount of good it has done in helping the education and instruction of the working people would be difficult to estimate. At the request of its managers an arrangement was made between the Apprentice's Library Company and the Free Quakers, in 1841, by which the Meeting House was rented to them for use as a library for a term of years, paying nominally fifty dollars per annum, but with the proviso that this money should not be paid to the land owners, but be invested in good and useful books each year, a list of which should be sent to the Free Quakers instead of rent ; in 1868, after several renewals of the original lease, a lease upon a small moneyed rent for a term of twenty-five years was entered into, which by subsequent renewals is still (1894) in force. The rent received from this source and the income generally has always been applied by the Society to the charitable relief of its own poor members, and then for the deserving poor of Philadelphia generally, so that this Society has helped the good work of instruction and education of many thousands of poor children, and has given assistance amounting to thousands of dollars to the poor of the city, which work is still being conducted. It pays no salaries, every one serves gratuitously. It has very few expenses. It makes no loud protestations. Its name is withdrawn from publication rather than advertised as to its good works, but the committee founded in 1829 has ever since worked faithfully to relieve the sufferings of the deserving poor of the city. Its labors during the winter just over (1894), and in the present distressed condition of the working people of our city, have been very great and are still continuing. So that the Society still lives as a true and active religious body, laboring on a charitable basis so far as it is able.

After the death of John Price Wetherill in 1853, the Society for a number of years held very few meetings ; the work being done by the Committee on Charity, but in 1882, John Price Wetherill, Jr., who had succeeded his father as clerk, called the Society together, and it was then resolved to hold a meeting at least once a year, on the first Wednesday of November; and this rule has since been followed, regular yearly meetings having ever since been held. This has very much revived the interest of the members, and the Society under the leadership of William H. Wetherill, its present clerk, is now increasing in numbers and activity.

On one point the members of the Society have certainly lived up to the precepts of their patriotic founders. In every war since the Revolution in which the United States has been engaged, involving resistance to invasion either by foreign enemy or domestic traitor, the members of this Society have done faithful service. In the revolt in Western Pennsylvania, known as the "Whiskey Insurrection," Col. Clement Biddle, rendered very active service. In the war of 1812, one certainly, and several more probably, served in the campaign for the defence of Baltimore and were present at the bombardment which inspired the writing of the National Hymn. Upon the breaking out of the war for the Union, the treasurer of the Society, too old for military service himself, raised and equipped a company of soldiers at his sole expense and presented them ready for service to the State; and several of the trustees and active members joined the Union army and served with distinction before Lynchburg, Petersburg, and Richmond; one of them, afterwards for several years treasurer of the Society, was taken prisoner, and survived not only the dangers of battle, but the sufferings of Libby Prison. When the soil of Pennsylvania was invaded by the Southern armies, they were present at the battle of Gettysburg, and Free Quakers helped to drive the enemy down, with terrible slaughter, from the "high-water mark of the Rebellion."

The youngest of its trustees, too young to serve in the war for the Union, has done active service in the National Guard of the State on the only occasions, since the rebellion, in which the service of soldiers has been needed in Pennsylvania: in the battle at the round house in Pittsburgh, in 1877, and at the siege of Homestead, in 1892.

Wherever the flag of the Union—the flag that was first made by a Free Quaker woman—has been fired upon by an enemy, Free Quakers have gone to defend the great republic that their forefathers risked " their lives, their fortunes, and their sacred honor " to found.

And these few historical notes may well close with the hope that this venerable Society may survive in its modest usefulness to see our country become, as is foretold on the tablet of its old meeting house, " the great *Empire* over all " this world."

Appendix No. 1.

AN ADDRESS

To those of the People called Quakers, who have been disowned for Matters Religious or Civil.

Friends and Fellow-Sufferers.—The scattered and distressed situation in which we have been for some time past, having occasioned great inconvenience to most of us, a small number of men, educated among the people called Quakers, as you have been, have met together and seriously considered our circumstances.

This separation has not been sought by, but forced upon, us, as the pride and folly of former churches, vainly attempting to abridge the rights of conscience, excommunicated their brethren from among them. And there appears no reasonable ground of expectation that we shall ever again be united to those who have disowned us; for they will not permit among them that Christian liberty of sentiment and conduct which all are entitled to enjoy, and which we cannot consent to part with. You know that many have been disowned by that people for no other cause than a faithful discharge of those duties which we owe to our country.

Thus situated, and acknowledging our dependence upon the Supreme Being, and the duty of public worship which we owe to him, we have lamented the loss of those advantages which arise from religious communion, and have feared still greater loss in this respect, to our children and families. And

47

therefore, although we know that "weakness is ours," and that difficulties and dangers surround us on every hand, confiding in the gracious promise of the Great Shepherd of his people, that he would "be with" even "two or three," wheresoever they are met together in his name, we have agreed, that as Friends and brethren, we will endeavor to support and maintain public meetings for religious worship.

We have no new doctrine to teach, nor any design of promoting schisms in religion. We wish only to be freed from every species of ecclesiastical tyranny, and mean to pay a due regard to the principles of our forefathers, and to their rules and regulations so far as they apply to our circumstances, and hope, thereby, to preserve decency and to secure equal liberty to all. We have no design to form creeds or confessions of faith, but humbly to confide in those sacred lessons of wisdom and benevolence, which have been left us by Christ and His apostles, contained in the holy scriptures ; and appealing to that divine principle breathed by the breath of God into the hearts of all, to leave every man to think and judge for himself, according to the abilities received, and to answer for his faith and opinions to him, who "seeth the secrets of all hearts," the sole Judge and sovereign Lord of conscience.

And feeling for you, as fellow-sufferers, a sympathy and brotherly affection, we think it our duty thus to communicate to you what we have done and are about to do, that you may, if you choose, partake with us in the blessings we seek and hope to obtain. As brethren indeed, united in affliction, "let us (agreeably to the counsel given by the Apostle Paul) "consider one another, to provoke unto love and to good "works; not forsaking the assembling of ourselves together, "as the manner of some is, but exhorting one another. And "so much the more as ye see the day approaching." Be en-

49

couraged, and let us meet together and ask bread from him in whose hand it is, with an humble hope, that he who giveth food "to the young ravens which cry" will provide also for us. And in this hope we salute you with unfeigned affection.

Signed in and on behalf of the meeting,

SAMUEL WETHERILL, JUN., *Clerk.*

PHILADELPHIA, *24th of the 4th Month, 1781.*

[PRINTED BY FRANCIS BAILEY.]

Appendix No. 2.

The Monthly Meeting of Friends, called by some

THE FREE QUAKERS,

(Distinguishing us from those of our Brethren who have disowned us.)

HELD AT PHILADELPHIA, THE 4TH DAY OF THE 6TH MONTH, 1781.

TO OUR FRIENDS AND BRETHREN IN PENNSYLVANIA, NEW JERSEY AND ELSEWHERE:—

Dear Friends.—Agreeable to the intimations given to you in our late "Address to those of the People called Quakers, who have been disowned for matters religious or civil," we have for some time past held two meetings for public worship on the first day of the week, and a meeting for conducting the business of the society, on the first second day of the week in each month. These meetings having afforded us great satisfaction, we shall continue them, with a firm hope that the blessing of heaven will, "as the dew of Hermon," descend in silence upon them.

In our deliberations on this subject we have been led to consider "That the Creator of man having bestowed upon individuals greater and less natural abilities and opportunities of improvement, a variety of sentiments respecting the duties which we owe to him necessarily arises among us, and it becomes essential to our happiness that we may perform those duties in that way which we think the most acceptable to him. And therefore when we contemplate the long and

earnest contest which has been maintained, and the torrents
of blood which, in other countries, have been shed in defence
of this precious privilege, we cannot but acknowledge it to
be a signal instance of the immediate care of a divine providence over the people of America, that he has in the present
great revolution, thus far established among us governments
under which no man, who acknowledges the being of a God,
can be abridged of any civil right on account of his religious
sentiments, while other nations, who see and lament their
wretched situation, are yet groaning under a grievous bondage. But government established upon these liberal, just, and
truly Christian principles, and wisely confined to the great
objects of ascertaining and defending civil rights, in avoiding
the possibility of wounding the conscience of any, must
necessarily leave some cases unprovided for, which come
properly under the care of religious societies. Hence we are
not only left at liberty to act agreeably to our sentiments,
but the necessity and obligation of establishing and supporting religious societies, are increased and strengthened.''

''We acknowledge the kindness of Providence in awakening us to a view of the deplorable situation in which we have
been: disowned and rejected by those among whom we have
been educated, and without a hope of being ever again united
to them: separated and scattered abroad, as if we had been
aliens in a strange land: the prospect of our situation has
indeed humbled us: but that mercy which, ''to an hair's-
breadth,'' covers the judgment seat of God, has preserved us,
and induced us to confide that he will care for us. Being
made sensible of the indispensable necessity of uniting
together, we have cast our care upon God, and depending upon
him for our support, conceive it to be a duty which we owe
to ourselves, our children, and families, to establish and sup-

port among us public meetings for religious worship, to appoint stated meetings for conducting the affairs of the Society, upon principles as liberal and enlarged toward one another, as those adopted by the State are toward all, and paying a due regard to the principles of our forefathers, and the spirit of the wise regulations established by them, to fix upon such rules as may enable us to preserve decency and good order: and among other things, to agree upon and make known a decent form of marriage, which may at once secure the rights of parents and children : and a mode of forming and preserving records of marriages, births, and burials.

For these purposes an essay of discipline, founded on that of our ancestors, has been formed, and laid before the meeting for business. A good degree of unanimity of sentiments thereupon has appeared among us ; but we have thought it proper to leave it open for further consideration, and thus to communicate to our friends what we are about to do, in order to avail ourselves of the advice and assistance of all who may kindly afford us their counsel. And we sincerely and earnestly desire that we may obtain and be guided by that "wisdom from above," which is sufficient to overcome every danger and difficulty which we may have to contend against, and finally unite us together, in a truly Christian fellowship, and in the bonds of peace. Signed by order of the Meeting,

SAMUEL WETHERILL, JR., *Clerk.*

Appendix No. 3.

From the Monthly Meeting of Friends, called by some,

THE FREE QUAKERS,

Held by Adjournment at Philadelphia, on the 9th Day of the 7th Month, 1781.

TO THOSE OF OUR BRETHREN WHO HAVE DISOWNED US:—

Brethren :—Among the very great number of persons whom you have disowned for matters religious and civil, a number have felt a necessity of uniting together for the discharge of those religious duties which we undoubtedly owe to God and to one another. We have accordingly met, and having seriously considered our situation, agreed to establish and endeavor to support, on the ancient and sure foundation, meetings for public worship, and meetings for conducting our religious affairs. And we rejoice in a firm hope, that as we humble ourselves before God, his presence will be found in them, and his blessing descend and rest upon them.

As you have by your proceedings against, separated your-selves from, us and declared that you have no unity with us, you have compelled us, however unwillingly, to become sepa-rate from you. And we are free to declare to you and the world, that we are not desirous of having any mistake which we happen to make laid to your charge; neither are we willing to have any of your errors brought as guilt against us. To avoid these, seeing that you have made the separation, we submit to have a plain line of distinction made between us and you. But there are some points which seem to require a comparison of sentiments between you and us, and some kind of decision to be made upon them. The property of that Society of which we and you were once joint members, is far from being inconsiderable, and we have done nothing which can afford even a pretension of our having forfeited our right therein.

Whether you have or have not a right to declare to the world your sentiments of the conduct of any individual; or whether you have or have not a right to sit in judgment over and pass sentence upon your Christian brethren differing in sentiment from you, although educated among you, are not questions now to be considered : but you having taken upon you to do those things, it remains only to be enquired, what are the consequences in law and equity of your having so done. Surely you will not pretend that our right is destroyed by those acts of yours. But we suggest to your consideration, Whether your conduct has or has not disqualified you to hold any part of that property? A serious and full consideration, of this question, and the critical and strikingly singular situation in which you stand, cannot injure you ; but it may, possibly, induce you to consider, with the more candour and readiness, what equity requires to be done by you toward us, or by us toward you ; and tend to a decision the most proper between brethren differing in sentiment one from another concerning their respective rights to property, yet each believing in him whose precept leads us, "to do unto others as we would they should do unto us."

Whatever may have been the consequences to yourselves, either of your conduct toward us as friends to the present revolution ; or of your conduct in other cases, less immediately respecting us, it seems to be unquestionably certain, that we have not done anything which can possibly forfeit our right. And we see no reason why we should surrender it up to you; but think it a duty incumbent on us to assert our claim.

As a place for holding our meetings for worship and meetings for business relative to the Society, is become necessary for us, since you have separated yourselves from us, by testifying against us, and thereby rendering it highly improper for us to appear among you, as one people, at your meetings, we think it proper for us to use, apart from you, one of the houses built by Friends in this city for those purposes. We are desirous of doing this in the most decent and unexceptionable manner, and we are willing to hear anything which you may choose to say on the subject. And therefore we thus invite you to the opportunity of doing it, and of shewing what degree of kindness and brotherly love toward us, still remains among you. We also mean to use the burial ground, whenever the occasion shall require it. For, however, the living may contend, surely the dead may lie peaceably together.

Lest any may infer too much from this representation, we think it proper explicitly to declare, that should our right to the property in question be found, in the law, to be superior to yours, from any consideration whatever, it is far, very far from our wish to seclude you from a joint participation with us in the use of it. Neither do we mean to solicit a decision in law, unless you by your conduct compel us to it.

We sincerely and earnestly desire to have this subject amicably, equitably and speedily adjusted, and request that this free communication of our sentiments may be made known to all who are usually consulted on business among you, and that, for this purpose, it may be read when you next meet together on religious business.

As Christians, labouring in some degree to forgive injuries, we salute you, and though rejected by you, we are your friends and brethren. Signed in and on behalf of the said Meeting, by,

SAMUEL WETHERILL, JR., Clerk.

The foregoing is copied from the original which was presented to Philadelphia Monthly Meeting. The following is endorsed on the back, in a handwriting evidently contemporaneous with the transaction.

The printed copy of a paper presented to the Monthly Meeting of Friends of Philadelphia, on the 27th of the 7th month, 1781, by Timothy Matlack, attended by Moses Bartram and White Matlack, the said T. M. saying "that they were appointed by a Monthly Meeting of "Friends, by some called the *Free Quakers*, to deliver the "same, and desired it might be read," and giving it to the Clerk it was laid on the table; upon which the said Timothy and his companions withdrew. Our meeting proceeded on our usual business, and at the close of it a Committee of five were appointed to inspect the Contents of the said paper, and Report their Judgment to a future meeting of the propriety of reading it in our meeting, who knowing that a paper of the like kind had been the same week delivered in the like manner to the Monthly Meetings for the northern and southern districts, and that a committee was appointed by each of those meetings also to consider the propriety of reading the same in those meetings: The three Committees in a few days met together and on comparing the several papers found they were exact copies of each other, and after deliberation on the contents, which were new and extraordinary, manifesting a disposition for Contest, and to give Friends trouble, it was thought advisable to call together a greater number of Friends selected from each of the Monthly Meetings, in order for further consultation on the subject, and that unanimity might prevail in our conclusion, who accordingly met, when the papers were again read, and after a full communication of sentiments the following report was agreed to be verbally delivered to each of our succeeding Monthly meetings—viz: " We have considered the contents of the

Copy of The Paper from Timothy Matlack and Company, presented to each of the Monthly Meetings of Friends in Philadelphia, published by themselves before either of the said meetings had concluded on an answer.

" papers presented to our last " meeting by Timothy Matlack and " others; and are of the judgment " that it is improper to be read in " the meeting, of which we think " the parties concerned will have " grounds to be convinced on a " cool and dispassionate reconsid- " eration of the nature and ten- " dency of the requisition they make."

Which Report being accordingly made to each of our Monthly Meetings in the eighth month and approved, it was agreed that the Clerk of each meeting should give the same verbally as the answer of the meeting to Timothy Matlack or either of the persons who attended with him if they should apply, or in case of an application to any other Friend, by any of the said persons, they should be referred for an answer to the Clerk of each meeting respectively, which was done accordingly by the said Clerks respectively to the said T. M.

Appendix No. 4.

Divers Freemen of the said Commonwealth beg leave to shew :—

That by the laws of the State, religious societies of people
are entitled to hold lots of ground for the purposes of erect-
ing thereon houses for worship and school houses, and for
burying grounds :—That the people called Quakers, in divers
parts of the State, have accordingly possessed themselves of
such estates and others: That your petitioners are not only by
birth, but some of us are, also, by subscription to the common
stock, and by subscription for particular purchases, etc., justly
entitled to the common use and possession of the estates so
held by the said people :—

That very great numbers of persons have been disowned by
the leading men of that society, on various pretences, especially during the present revolution; And omitting very many
of those pretences, we beg leave to mention the following, to
wit. :—

Some have been disowned for affirming allegiance to the
State in compliance with the laws ;—and their elders and overseers have proposed and insisted on a renunciation of that
allegiance, as a condition of re-union with them.

Some for holding offices under the State, and some for holding offices under the United States.

Many for bearing arms in defence of our invaded country,

58

although the laws of the State enjoined and required it of them.

And some have been disowned for having paid the taxes required of them by law !

That many so disowned have been greatly distressed thereby. They felt and acknowledged the duty of public worship, and anxiously desired, for themselves and their families, the benefits which arise out of a performance of that duty. To join with other religious societies would have done violence to their religious principles, and to join with those who had disowned them, was evidently improper: therefore, they agreed to worship, apart from those who had disowned them, in the meeting houses to which they deem themselves justly entitled. For this end decent representations to the several monthly meetings of Philadelphia, and to the yearly meeting, have been made ; these have been rejected without a reading. The key of one of the meeting houses not then in use, hath been requested and refused, and the names of the committees by whom these measures have been advised, have been concealed from us, whereby, we have not only been deprived of the use of those houses to which we are entitled, but are prevented even from conferring with those who withhold it from us.

That certain men among those people have assumed and exercised a pretended right to refuse, or to *grant as of favour*, at their discretion and pleasure, the interment of the dead in the burying ground granted in common to their and our ancestors, of which two contrasted instances are alleged—One man, who died in the service of the United States, was denied the right of burial, "because he had borne arms and been concerned in war." Another man, having no pretension of right, who had been convicted of an attempt to bribe the pilots of the State to conduct the British fleet into our harbour, condemned, hanged, and buried in other ground, was long after taken up, and interred, *by their order*, among our friends !

That those people thus assume and exercise, not only a power of condemning and publicly censuring men for their obedience to the laws of the land, but, in effect, decree and execute forfeitures against them for such obedience.

That, connected with many of the members of that society by the strongest ties, we have no desire to injure them ; and mention those facts for the sole purpose of shewing to this honourable house our true situation.

That, however painful it is to be held up by those people to the world as "Heathen men," and as being "cut off, by the sword of the spirit, from the Church of Christ," confiding in the justice of that cause in which we are engaged, we solemnly appeal for a decision on this point to the Great Arbiter of heaven and earth. And, respecting the said property, con-sidering the case of those so disowned as arising out of a great revolution which the laws have not provided for, and proper for the consideration of the legislature,

We pray this honorable house, in whose justice and wisdom we confide, will grant leave to bring in a bill for recognizing the right of persons disowned by the people called Quakers, to hold in common with others of that society, the meeting houses, school houses, burying grounds, lots of land, and other the estates held by that people as a religious society, and to recognize their right to search, examine, and take copies of the records, books and papers, of the said society, from time to time, for the purpose of ascertaining such estates, proving marriages, ascertaining descents and securing their rights, and other purposes as they may have occasion ; and to enable those so disowned to purchase and hold such estates as other religious societies are by law entitled to hold and enjoy.

And your petitioners, as in duty bound, will pray, etc.

SIGNATURES OF PETITIONERS INDORSED ON THE PETITION.

THOS. CRISPIN,	JOSEPH GOVETT,	CADL. DICKINSON,
THO. BRYAN,	JNO. RICHARDSON,	CALEB HEWES,
ABR. SHOEMAKER,	THOS. COATS,	J. FISHER,
ROBT. JONES,	THOS. HOPKINS,	WM. FISHER JR.,
JOSEPH OGDEN,	EVAN EVANS,	ABR. ROBERTS,
SAM'L. HOWELL,	MOSES BARTRAM,	JOHN KNIGHT,
EDWD. HESTON,	JNO. MORRIS,	NATHL. ALLEN,
JAMES BARTRAM,	JAS. PEARSON,	JOHN BELL,
JOHN BARTRAM,	GO. CHANDLER,	SAML. MORRIS,
JONA. PASCHALL,	JAMES DELAPLAINE,	BENJ. PASCHALL,
HENRY HAYES,	NATHAN GIBSON,	JOSEPH STILES,
J. PEARSON,	WM. DARRAGH,	PET. THOMSON,
JOS. PEARSON,	J. MUSGRAVE,	ISSAC HOWELL,
SAM'L. SMITH,	ARON MUSGRAVE,	BENJ. SAY,
MATT. ASH,	SAM'L WETHERILL,	NATHL. BROWNE,
JONA. BONSALL,	WHITE MATLACK,	JNO. PARRISH JR.,
JNA. ASH,	EDW. EVANS,	WM. MILNOR,
JOS. BONSALL,	TIMO. MATLACK,	SAML. ROBBINS,
JOSHUA BONSALL,	THS. RENSHAW,	CLEMT. BIDDLE,
JOSH. OGDEN JR.,	RICH'D SOMERS,	DAVID EVANS,
	WM. CRISPIN.	

[The petition was presented to the legislature on December 21, A, D., 1781, and ordered to lie on the table.]

Appendix No. 5.

PHILADELPHIA, Ninth Month, 7th, 1782.

The following Memorial and Address was presented to the Assembly soon after the date of it, and is entered on the Journals of the House in the Second Month last; a recent attack of Isaac Howell and White Matlack in a remonstrance to the House now sitting, of a like nature with the petition to which this Memorial is an answer, makes it necessary to be more extensively published.

TO THE GENERAL ASSEMBLY OF PENNSYLVANIA:—

An Address and Memorial on Behalf of the People Called Quakers.

Being informed that a petition was presented to you at your last sitting, signed by some persons residing in Philadelphia and parts adjacent, which affected the reputation and interest of our religious society, and, on our application, being in-dulged with a copy thereof, we find it is intended to arraign the discipline established among us, and artfully designed to impress your minds with unfavorable sentiments, by misrepresentations and injurious charges against us which we hope we are able to confute to your satisfaction, so as to obviate the evil intentions of this attack upon our religious and civil rights and liberties; and therefore, apprehend it not improper to offer to your consideration, a few remarks as briefly as the nature of the subject will admit.

62

The doctrine and order deliberately and conscientiously received and settled, by the united concurrence of our religious society, we have at all times held it our indispensable duty to maintain by the gospel methods of instruction, advice and admonition, and in cases of disorderly walking, which have a tendency to infringe upon the peace and unity of the church, we proceed no further than to a suspension of a close communion with the parties offending, or as occasion might call for it, to declare that they being departed from the unity of the body, are no longer of it.

We apprehend, that when any religiously united body hath in its collective capacity, according to the understanding received from the holy spirit, and agreeable to the holy scriptures, fixed the terms of its communion, it has a right in all points it deems material, to see that they are preserved inviolate by its members, and to acknowledge or reject any according to their faithfulness or unfaithfulness thereunto, and where it judges any have justly forfeited their membership, to declare so; otherwise, litigious and refractory members might render the church a stage of perpetual contention and confusion; or, as a kingdom divided against itself, which cannot stand. For its own peace and preservation, therefore, it can do no less than to " withdraw itself from every brother that walketh disorderly," 2 Thess., iii and 3, which can be done by no means more proper than by declaring its disunion with them.

This is the ultimate process of the people called Quakers, which is not intended by them for the punishment of any, but for keeping the church clear from disorder.

Rules are necessary to the support of order in religious as well as civil societies. There must be some power in the collective body, which is not in every particular singly to answer the end of order. This cannot be less than a power to accept or reject particular members according to the suitableness or unsuitableness of their conduct with its doctrines and rules. The nature of society and the fitness of things require thus much and our discipline extends no further. It intrudes not upon the civil rights of its members, affects no secular authority over their persons or property; but leaves them in a reasonable freedom either to continue in membership by a conduct agreeable to our principles and rules, or to separate from us if they think fit; nor are any prohibited from assembling with us in our meetings for public worship, which it is well known are held openly, and free to all sober people.

The nature of society requires unity and harmony. A continued infraction of the terms of its communion, is not only a continual interruption to the peace of it, but has a tendency to its dissolution; hence it behooves every regular united body, to support the observance of its rules among its members, for its own peace and preservation; sensible of this, the apostle in his epistle to the Romans writes thus: "I beseech you brethren, mark them which cause divisions "and offences, contrary to the doctrine which ye have "learned, and avoid them."—This a church cannot do but by clearing itself of them, which is a necessary exertion of gospel discipline, towards those who might give disturbance to it, or "by fair speeches deceive the hearts of the simple."

Besides God's exterior dispensation of his written law, he still condescends according to his gracious promise, to teach his people immediately by his spirit in their hearts; this is the true basis of the right of private judgment, and as this is a privilege sacred to every man, so it is to every religious society, no one of which is entitled to impose upon another, in matters of doctrine or order; neither has any individual a right to impose himself upon it, contrary to its established rules.

The respectable John Locke saith, " No man by nature "is bound unto any particular church or sect, but every one "joins himself voluntarily to that society in which he believes "he has found that profession and worship which is truly "acceptable to God. As no man is bound to any church " against his particular conscience, neither is any church " bound to any man against that rule and order established " therein, according to its collective conscience. I hold " that no church is bound by the duty of toleration, to re- " tain any such person in her bosom, as after admonition, "continues to offend against the laws of the society. For " these being the condition of communion, and the bond of " the society, if the breach of them were permitted without " animadversion, the society would immediately be thereby "dissolved." Let. on Toleration, 4 ed. Pa. 10 and 13. Liberty of consciences is every man's undoubted right, and no less the right of every religious society, and as no man ought to be forcibly imposed upon in that respect, neither should any religious society suffer itself to be imposed upon against its judgment by any man, whatever his pretence may be ; nor is that man who attempts it, doing as he would be done by in such attempt ; or shewing that regard to the conscience of the body that he claims to his own. The religious liberty of a person consists not in a power to impose himself upon any religious society, against the rules of its communion, but in a freedom to join himself to one whose rules, doctrine and worship are conformable to his conscience, or to disjoin himself from one where all or any of them are not so.

Every one who hath espoused opinions different from those

5

of the people called quakers is at liberty to leave them, and join himself to any other people ; this cannot be stiled a hard or unjust measure ; freedom of enquiry is allowed, and liberty of action is allowed so far as can be consistent with the nature and peace of society, which cannot be properly supported, if its members are suffered to live in the breach of its rules and orders without any animadversion.

The intention of our discipline is not a dominion over the faith, or an abridgment of the just liberty of any ; it seeks not the hurt of any, but the good of all ; and that purity of manners, love, peace, and harmony may be preserved throughout the whole body on the basis of truth. The society proceeds no further in any case than it believes itself necessarily obliged to do, as a Christian body. And in showing its disunity with such of its members as violate its rules and orders, it is warranted by the laws of the land ; it having as we have understood, been also publicly declared by learned judges in courts of judicature in Great Britain, to be the common privilege of all societies of tolerated dissenters ; and we hope the same reason will equally avail in America.

Now we do not deny that many of the petitioners stand disunited from religious membership with us, and divers of them have been so from ten to twenty years past and upwards, which separation on our part has proceeded from necessity, and not of choice, nor on mere " pretences " as they suggest ; the causes which produced it, for their sakes we do not care to revive, unless they should make it unavoidable ; there are also in the number, such who were never acknowledged among us, if not some who have had no claim to such right.

We presume not to cut off any " from the Church of Christ " ; for if a member of the natural body be cut off, it is impossible to unite it again, so as sensibly to communicate with, and be restored to its proper use in the body. The case of one disowned by us should rather be considered as a member who may be restored, having instances of many, who through divine mercy, becoming sensible of their deviation in conduct and the propriety of our proceedings towards them, have returned into christian fellowship with us, to their satisfaction and ours.

Nor are any persons disowned by "leading men," among us; but if a member thinks himself aggrieved by the united judgment of a monthly meeting, he has the right of appealing to the quarterly meeting, as also to our yearly meeting, and it is our practice to notify the party concerned, of his having this privilege, that he may embrace it, if he thinks proper; and in these several meetings, that every acknowledged member has liberty to judge and speak.

Having heretofore expressed our sentiments and principles on the subject of war, and relating to tests, particularly in our memorial to the late assembly on the 4th of the 11th month, 1779, which is entered on their minutes; we are unwilling now to detain your attention on these points, prefering to manifest that a peaceable demeanour, and passive submission to the laws, where our conscience to God restrains us from active compliance, are a greater security to government than verbal declarations; the solemnity of which, is found in too many instances to be no longer regarded than it suits the convenience of those who make them.

We know not of any of our members being disowned, for the payment of taxes, for the support of government, nor is there any rule of our discipline that requires it.

Had the promoters of the petition shewn that regard to candour, which becomes men professing a concern for the cause of religion, they would have given a different relation of the "contrasted instances," (as they term them) of the interment of two dead bodies; the first which we suppose they allude to, had been a person who made no profession with us, he resided and died several miles distant from the city, and was little known to the persons to whom application was first made for an order to the grave-digger, which occasioned some enquiry to be necessary, and tho' the appliers were answered by them, that their application was judged improper to be complied with, yet three of the relations of the deceased were timely told, that the request would be allowed: which as they did not accept, it was supposed that his family found it more convenient to bury him in a grave-yard in the neighborhood of their residence.

There was an application made for the interment of the other, at the time of his execution, but as he made no profession with us, as well as in consideration·of the occasion of his death, it was disallowed. The body being afterwards taken up and removed to our ground, was known to very few at that time, but as soon as it was heard of, caused great uneasiness to our brethren in the city, who manifested their disapprobation of the unadvised measure; so that their misrepresentation of these occurrences must proceed from wrong information, or a view to prejudice us, and increase the number of subscribers to their petition; while they are silent on the methods they took by threats of forcibly entering the grave-yard, for the interment of two children, to which they had no reason to suspect any hesitation would be made.

The care of our burying-ground in the city is committed to persons appointed by our monthly meetings, to consider the propriety of applications, and give permissions to the grave-digger for interments within their respective limits. An assertion therefore, that any individuals among us " have "assumed a right to grant, as matter of favour, the liberty of burial," is far from being true.

The lot of ground which is now our grave-yard in Philadelphia, was a donation of a worthy member of our religious society, at the very early settlement of the city, for the use of the people called quakers; who are and shall be in union and fellowship with the yearly meeting of the said people, for a burying place, and granted to certain persons in trust for that purpose; nevertheless, it hath been the general practice not to refuse those who have, near the close of life, desired to be interred there, whether in profession with us or not; and the records of our burials will sufficiently evidence, that the number interred of such, who were not members, is nearly equal to, if not greater than, those in membership with us cavilling on this account can therefore have no just foundation.

That we possess some estate, on which houses for public worship, and other necessary buildings, are erected, we acknowledge, and that they have been justly acquired, and are legally held we must likewise assert, as also that the income arising, tho' far short of what some would make out, is carefully applied for the relief and maintenance of the poor, the instruction of their children, and other benevolent purposes, for which they were originally given or purchased, which, with the frequent contributions among ourselves, for the like uses, must be allowed to be a public benefit, and saving to the community at large in which we dwell, as we also contribute our full proportion to the support of the public poor.

The papers, by the petitioners termed, decent representations, which they suggest were treated with slight and neglect, were committed to the inspection of a number of friends (in the same manner as all other papers, so offered, are) and reported to be improper to be read in our meetings, of which, on their enquiry they were duly informed.

Whenever application has been made for transcripts from our records for the ascertaining descents, proving of births, marriages or burials, and other purposes, for securing the rights of individuals, they have always been readily allowed, and certified copies given without fee or reward, or the originals produced, when necessary, so that a law to recognize what has never been denied, appears to be entirely needless.

The petitioners by their several publications, their present petition as well as their general conduct, openly declare that they do not agree with us in the fundamentals of our faith, and what has been the uniform practice from our first becoming a united society; but if they really mean by their new association, the promotion of piety and virtue and the edification of each other in love and good works, it would be commendable not to attempt to establish themselves on a violation of the commandment which enjoins, " thou shalt not covet thy neighbor's house, or anything that is thy neighbor's." And is equally forcible against coveting to obtain that from a religious body, to which they have no right in law or justice, and at the same time profess " they have no desire to injure them," which contradictions, had they duly considered, would have occasioned more caution and modesty in their solemn appeal " to the great arbiter of heaven and earth," when their designs, however disguised by plausible " pretences," are so easily discoverable to men.

The prayer of the petitioners will we think not only appear unprecedented and unreasonable, but, if granted, may establish a precedent injurious to every religious society, by restraining the right of disowning any of their members even for the most flagrant immoralities and other offences. And therefore we hope and trust that on mature and deliberate consideration of the nature and tendency of so singular a petition, you will judge it most just and expedient to answer the petitioners as Gallio answered the Jews, when they accused the apostle Paul before him. Acts xviii, 12 to 16.

We are your respectful Friends,

Signed on behalf and by
   direction of a Meeting
   of the Representatives of
   the said People called   JOHN DRINKER, *Clerk.*
   Quakers held at Phila-
   delphia, the 18th 1st
   Month, 1782.

Appendix No. 6.

The Memorial and Remonstrance of Isaac Howell
and White Matlack, on behalf of themselves and
others, who have been disowned by the
People called Quakers, etc.,
Respectfully sheweth.

That in a law of this state passed on the Thirteenth day of
June, 1777, entitled, "An Act obliging the male white inhabi-
tants of this state to give assurances of allegiance to the
same," etc., it is declared that, "allegiance and protection
are reciprocal, and that those who will not bear the former,
are not (and ought not to be) entitled to the latter:" the
first part of which declaration is the great and solid basis
upon which civil society is established. That the good people
of Pennsylvania considering the said declaration, not as un-
meaning words, but as holding out and inviting all to a most
important compact, essential to their well being: and which
on the part of the state, was intended faithfully and inviol-
ably to be preserved, solemnly gave those "assurances of allegiance," which entitled them to protection. That your
memorialists, being among those who have thus entered this
important compact, consider this right of protection thus
gained to be in value beyond estimation. And that as the
state is bound by the most solemn engagements to afford that

protection to those who have given allegiance; so it is the indispensable duty of every man to claim and assert his title to it whenever any of his rights are invaded.

That your memorialists justly considering this honorable house as the representatives of the state, from which they were of right entitled to claim protection, presented their petition, representing in effect, that great numbers of freemen had been disowned by the people called Quakers, under various pretences, especially during the struggle of this great revolution, and stating four distinct cases ; viz.

They have been disowned for having given allegiance to the state in compliance with the laws.

For holding offices under the state, and under the united states.

For bearing of arms in the defence of our invaded country alth° the laws of the state enjoined and required it of us.

And for the payment of taxes required by law.

And they further represented, in effect, that a number of persons so disowned and cut off from religious communion and fellowship with those among whom they had been educated, collecting together, and being sensible of the duty of public worship, agreed to worship apart from those who had disowned them, in the meeting houses built by our common ancestors, at such times as not to interrupt or prevent those who had disowned them, from a common use of the same houses :—That the peaceable means adopted to obtain for that purpose the use of those meeting houses had been ineffectual, and treated by the leaders of the monthly meeting of Philadelphia, and others, with a total disregard :—That certain men among them, assumed and exercised a pretended right to refuse, or to grant as of favour, at their discretion and pleasure, the interment of the dead in the burying ground granted

74

in common to their and our ancestors, and gave instances of
the most insulting and intolerable abuse of that assumed
power ; that the petitioners were then ready to give the most
full, clear, and unequivocal testimony of each and every fact
stated in the said representation. That the said petitioners
conceiving themselves of right entitled to protection, and
their case a new one, "arising out of a great revolution which
the laws have not provided for," and therefore "proper for
the consideration of the legislature," and confiding in the
justice and wisdom of the house, prayed leave to bring in a
bill, in effect, to supply the deficiency of the laws, in a case
which had not, and scarce possibly could have been foreseen,
and thereby secure to them the rights and privileges which
were thus withheld from them. A prayer so just and reason-
ble, it was hoped and expected would have been readily
granted ; but the petitioners were abashed when they read in
the minutes of the house, that their petition was "referred to
the committee of grievances;" as if their complaint had been
against officers acting under the government, and abusing the
authorities of it.

That your memorialists having seen the "address and
memorial on behalf of the people called Quakers" signed
by "John Drinker, clerk," which has been presented to the
general assembly, remark, that the most material facts stated
in the aforesaid petition, are admitted, and others equivocally
denied, that the addressers assert their right of disowning,
threaten to publish the causes for which many of the petitioners had been disowned, and refer this honorable house to
a decision which they hope the house will think "a just and
expedient" answer to our said petition.

Your memorialists will not waste the time of this honourable
house in minute observations upon an address artfully calcu-

lated to lead from the point in question, which is not an enquiry whether religious societies may disown their members for immoral acts ; but whether a religious society, disowning their members for complying with the laws of their country, in those great and important points on which its liberty and happiness essentially and absolutely depend, may at their will and pleasure, withhold from the persons so disowned, the use of the places of worship, burial grounds, etc., provided for them by their ancestors : and in case of any society, under pretence of religion, attempting so to do whether the state is not bound to make laws to secure those rights to such persons as have given allegiance to it, and thereby prevent the injustice attempted against them.

How far the quotation from Locke, cited in the address will apply to these questions, your memorialists are well content that this honourable house shall decide, without a single remark thereon from us, and on the threat of publishing the causes of disowning, we shall make no other observation, than this single truth, that the subscribers to the said petition, are friends to the revolution, of established character, many of them well known to the members of this honourable house, and have nothing to fear from such threats.

Your memorialists observe, that the interment of Molesworth, alluded to in the petition, is said in the address to have been " known to a very few at the time," but the fact is otherwise : he was interred by a formal written order, signed by the overseers, and his funeral was attended by a very great number of the people of that society—which is too notorious to need proof,—and respecting the fact of their refusing to inter another person because he had borne arms and been concerned in war, we are ready to give the clearest evidence; and as to threats of violence in the interment of two children, it is un-

true, and we are ready to shew, that far from proposing anything of that sort, the first magistrate of the city, was called
upon to witness, that no riot or unlawful violence of any kind
was committed.

The decision referred to in the address, and recommended
as a just and expedient answer from this honourable house to
the petitioners, we hope and confide will be well considered
before it is adopted : we pray leave to recite it ; it is in the following words : " And when Gallio was the deputy of Achaia,
" the Jews made insurrection with one accord against Paul,
" and brought him to the judgment seat ; saying, This fellow
" persuadeth men to worship God contrary to the law, and
" when Paul was now about to open his mouth, Gallio said
" unto the Jews, if it were a matter of wrong, or wicked
" lewdness, O ye Jews, would that I should bear with you.
" But if it be a question of words and names, and of your
" law look ye to it, for I will be no judge of such matters ; and
" he drave them from the judgment seat." Acts xviii, 12 to
16.

We ask in what part of our petition have we charged the
people called Quakers with " persuading men to worship God
contrary to law," or what " questions of words and names "
have we proposed ? What is there contained in the petition
on which such insinuated charges can in any sort be founded?
the complaint thereto made is clearly stated to be a " matter
of wrong" which Gallio declares ought to be heard, and we
pray leave to make a few short remarks on the answer recommended.

We ask, what have the petitioners done that should induce
the honourable house to drive them from before it ? The
sentence of Gallio stands approved because the Jews had done
wrong to Paul ; but what wrong have we done to the ad-

dressers? they do not even pretend any : but suppose the case before Gallio had been parallel with ours : that the Roman empire had been invaded, that the Jews had countenanced or abetted the enemy, while they were desolating the country with fire and sword, that Paul born a jew had taken part with the empire and exposed his life in its defence ; that the Jews for that reason, but under the pretence of religion, had expelled Paul from among them, and secluded him from the occasional use of the sepulchres of his ancestors, and other rights descended to him, and that thus circumstanced, Paul had appealed to Cæsar's deputy for protection, and that instead of affording him protection, Gallio had driven Paul from before the judgment seat ; what would Cæsar have said to Gallio for such a flagrant abuse and foolish violation of his trust ? Would not Cæsar have put Gallio to death? If the meeting for sufferings appointed by that part of the people called Quakers, who have disowned us, think it their duty to offer their advice to this honourable house, as to what answer it shall give to our petition, they ought to consider this case. But we should deem ourselves highly criminal, if we entertained the most distant thought, that this honourable house would adopt so unjust a sentence.

We have hitherto forborne to urge this matter upon this honourable house, interesting as it is to us, because of the unusual weight of business which has pressed upon the house : but we should be wanting in due respect, if we permitted the subject to remain in its present state, so as to leave an impression of doubt upon the minds of any, whether this house would extend to the petitioners that protection to which they are of right so clearly entitled.

But if those facts stated in the petition, and conceded in the address and memorial, are not deemed amply sufficient to induce the house to grant the prayer of the petition, we are ready to prove every fact alleged by us : and if those are not deemed sufficient, we suggest the following, which will place the conduct of the leaders of the society of the people called Quakers, attached to the cause of our enemies in its true point of view: we say, of the leaders, because it is a well known fact, that a great number of the independent part of that people, have under peculiar difficulties arising from their situation and connections, done honour to themselves by the most spirited efforts in the cause of their country.

Cadwallader Dickinson of Philadelphia was disowned for sitting as a juryman on the trial of John Roberts and Abraham Carlile, on a charge of high treason, of which they were convicted, and for which they suffered death, although he was requested to serve on that duty by a relation of one of those men.   On the other hand the persons so charged, found guilty and executed, or one of them, were expressly acknowledged to be members of the said society, and were not disowned for their treason.

We are ready to offer to this honourable house the testimony of a man of established good reputation, in support of the following fact, viz :

A testimony, as they term it, prepared for disowning a member for bearing of arms, and read in a meeting of business in Philadelphia, was so expressed as to censure the joining of the American army: it was remarked by one present, that·the bearing of arms was a sufficient cause for disowning, but that the joining of either side in the contest need not make any part of the charge.   To this it was replied, that the person charged, had by joining the American army, added to the fault of bearing arms, the crimes of treason and rebellion. Whereupon another person present expressed great concern, that such a sentiment should be delivered in the meeting, and at the same time declaring, that he considered the government of the state to be so far established, as to claim his respect and acknowledgement. Whereupon an eminent speaker in that society declared "That he hoped there was "not another man in that meeting who entertained a like "sentiment; that he (the person who had expressed that "sentiment) put him in mind of the vicar of Bray:" here the debate ended and the words censuring the joining of the American army were continued, as expressing the sentiments of that people! We have forborne to give the names of the persons concerned in this transaction, because we do not wish to alledge them as charges against individuals, but we are ready to give them, whenever we shall be required so to do.

The public testimonies of those people, published at different times, are known to all, and need not be here recited; but it is perhaps not known to many, that those people in their meetings for business, quarterly, half-yearly, and yearly, put the following query, in effect: Are friends careful not to defraud the King of his dues? and we believe this query is still continued! And it is worthy of remark, that, even in the address and memorial to this honourable house, they avoid any acknowledgement of the right of government, and speak of them as men "who are in the exercise of the powers of government," and yet notwithstanding such strong and full evidences, these people have the assurance publicly to declare, that "no just cause of offence will be found against them in the general:" appear before this honourable house, and not only claim its protection, while they withhold their allegiance and disclaim the revolution and government; but also claim a right of punishing those who yield allegiance, by depriving them of their rights descending from their ancestors.

They have even made it a condition of persons having taken allegiance to the state, marrying among them, that that allegiance shall be renounced, and the certificate thereof returned. Of which strange fact we are ready to give full proof. These men, we say, come before this honourable house, claim the right of disfranchising hundreds of the freemen of the state, for having faithfully discharged, in the time of her distress, the great duties which they owed to their country, and withhold from them their property, peculiarly valued by all men, and appropriating that property to their own sole use ; and when appeal is made to the legislature of the state, and protection asked, in terms the most decent and respectful, these men take upon them to recommend as a "proper" and "expedient" answer that we should "be driven from before" you, unheard. And, if possible, to add to the insult, while they withhold our just rights, calmly recommend us to observe the command, which forbids to "covet that which is our neighbour's."

What people of any age or country, have ever yet been found, who would suffer their houses of worship, and the bones of their ancestors to be violated and torn from them without the most desperate resistance ? We know of none. Nor do we know what we have done, or omitted to do, that should induce any to think that we should on the present occasion, be more tame and submissive than the most abject of mankind. In order to shew our real situation we beg leave to recite a recent fact :—a minister of the gospel, long in high estimation among the people called Quakers, was disowned by that people in the state of Massachusetts Bay, for no other cause than for having published, as his opinion, that that people, consistent with their religious profession may pay their taxes for the support of government : came to this state on a religious visit to those who have been disowned here, and having appointed a meeting for worship, to be held in the meeting house at Merion, the key was obtained from the keeper, and the house opened for that purpose, when two of the leading members of that meeting came about the time appointed for holding the. meeting, locked up the house, took away the key and prevented the meeting from being held : yet so late as the years 1777 and 1778, all the meeting houses in the state were opened to a preacher from England, then here, although it is generally understood that he considered, and on all occasions, public and private, spoke of the present revolution as a rebellion. If indeed your memorialists are mistaken in their claim of right to protection in the enjoyment of the meeting houses and burial grounds obtained by their ancestors, and that those of the people called Quakers, who have discountenanced the present revolution, have a divine right, or any other right, to supercede the law of the land, and to punish those who pay obedience to it, by depriving them of any of their rights and privileges, let it be so said : but your memorialists think it their duty to re-iterate the prayer of their former petition.

"We pray this honourable house, in whose justice and
"wisdom we confide, will grant leave to bring in a bill for
"recognizing the right of persons disowned by the people
"called Quakers, to hold in common with others of that soci-
"ety, the meeting houses, school houses, burying grounds,
"lots of land, and other the estates held by that people as a
"religious society, and to recognize their right to search,
"examine, and take copies of the records, books, and papers
"of the said society from time to time, for the purpose of
"ascertaining descents, and securing their rights and other
"purposes as they may have occasion, and to enable those so

6

" disowned to purchase and hold such estates as other relig-
" ious societies are by law entitled to hold and enjoy."

And whatever may be the determination of this honourable
house in other respects, they further pray, that this memorial
and remonstrance may be entered upon the journals of the
house, in order that hereafter, we may have recourse to authentic records for proof of our having thus early made a *claim of
right*, and done everything in our power to do consistent with
the peace of civil society for obtaining *a declaration of that
right by law ;* that from authentic record, the People of Pennsylvania, and the states in union, the literati of Europe, and
posterity, may judge of our situation and be enabled justly
to decide upon such further measures as may hereafter become
necessary to obtain those rights, which we can never consent
to have coercively taken away, or withheld from us.

Signed, Isaac Howell,

White Matlack.

[From an Ancient Printed Copy of the Journal of the House. This was
Presented 21st of 8th Month, 1782.]

Appendix No. 7.

To the Representatives of the Freemen of the Commonwealth of Pennsylvania, in General Assembly met,
Respectfully Sheweth :

That the subscriber and White Matlack on behalf of themselves and others presented a memorial and remonstrance to
the Honourable House on the 21st of August last, praying
that a law might be passed for declaring the rights of Persons
disowned by the people called Quakers, and other purposes
Expressed in said memorial.

The Honorable House then took the said memorial into
their consideration and appointed a "committee to confer
with the memorialists, Examine the facts set forth in the
memorial, and report to the House." That as the above
order of the House was only in part complied with, they hoped
the house would have entered on a further consideration
of this business before them in the earlier part of the
present sitting: but finding it still omitted, they pray
the Honorable house will now resume the further consideration of the said memorial and remonstrance, and
grant to your memorialists that protection to which they
are of right so clearly entitled.

In addition to former petitions they beg leave to present
the inclosed.

(signed) Isaac Howell.

[It was Probably Presented Early in March, 1783.]

84

The enclosure was as follows :—

TO THE REPRESENTATIVES OF THE FREEMEN OF THE COMMONWEALTH OF PENNSYLVANIA, IN GENERAL ASSEMBLY MET.

We, the subscribers, disowned by the people called Quakers, do hereby certify that we request that a law may be passed for declaring the rights of persons disowned by that people and other purposes expressed in the memorial of Isaac Howell and White Matlack, and presented to the Honorable House.

(Signed).

SAM'L WETHERILL, JR.,
JAMES BOONE, JR.,
SAMUEL FOULKE,
MOSES BARTRAM,
BENJAMIN SAY,
JONATHAN SCHOLFIELD,
ABRAHAM ROBERTS,
CLEMENT BIDDLE,
PETER THOMPSON,
EDWARD POLE,
JAMES PEARSON,

EDWARD EVANS,
RICHARD SOMERS,
JONATHAN DRAPER,
THOMAS ROSS, JR.,
JOHN BUCKMAN, JR.,
ISAAC HESTON,
RICHARD LEEDOM,
NATHANIEL BROWNE,
CADW. DICKINSON,
AB. SHOEMAKER,
THOMAS WRIGHT,
WILLIAM MATLACK,

THOMAS HOPKINS,
JOHN CHAPMAN,
JOSHUA ELY,
JAMES POTTER,
NATHANIEL ELLICOT,
ENOCH BETTS,
SAML. SMITH,
THOMAS DYER,
TIMOTHY TAYLOR,
STACY TAYLOR,
ABNER BUCKMAN,
JOSEPH LEES.

Appendix No. 8.

Copy of the Deed from Samuel Wetherill and wife to Christopher Marshall and others, Trustees.

This Indenture, Made the tenth day of the seventh month, called July, in the year of our Lord one thousand seven hundred and eighty-three between Samuel Wetherill, Jr., of the City of Philadelphia in the State of Pennsylvania, Carpenter, and Sarah his wife, of the one part, and Christopher Marshall, Sr., of the said city, gentleman; Nathaniel Brown, of the said city, blacksmith; Isaac Howell, of the said city, Esquire; Peter Thomson, of the said city, conveyancer; Moses Bartram, of the said city, druggist; Jonathan Scholfield, of the said city, shopkeeper; Benjamin Say, of the said city, practitioner in physic; Joseph Warner, of the said city, lastmaker; and Abraham Roberts, of the said city, grocer, of the other part.

Whereas, John Dunlap, of said city, printer, and Elizabeth his wife, by indenture of the fifth day of this instant month called July, for the consideration therein mentioned did grant and confirm unto the said Samuel Wetherill, his heirs and assigns, all that certain lot or piece of ground, situate on the south side of Mulberry or Arch street and west side of Fifth street from the river Delaware in the said city, containing in breadth on the said Mulberry street forty-eight feet, and in length or depth one hundred feet, bounded northward with the said Mulberry street, eastward with the said Fifth street,

85

southward with another lot of ground granted by the said
John Dunlap and wife to the said Samuel Wetherill, and westward with ground formerly of William Hudson, and now or
late of Joseph Wharton and Hannah his wife : Together with
the appurtenances to hold to him, the said Samuel Wetherill,
his heirs and assigns forever, subject to the payment of a certain yearly rent-charge or sum of four pounds eight shillings
lawful money of Pennsylvania, as the same should hereafter
grow due and payable, as in and by the said recited Indenture,
Relation being thereunto had, at large appears. Now *This
Indenture Witnesseth*, That the said Samuel Wetherill and
Sarah his wife, as well for and in consideration of the sum of
ten shillings in specie unto them well and truly paid by the
said Christopher Marshall, Nathaniel Brown, Isaac Howell,
Peter Thomson, Moses Bartram, Jonathan Scholfield, Benjamin Say, Joseph Warner, and Abraham Roberts, at or before
the sealing and delivering hereof, the Receipt whereof is hereby acknowledged, as for divers other good causes and valu-
able considerations them hereunto specially moving. Have
granted, bargained, sold, released, and confirmed, and by
these presents do grant, bargain, sell, release, and confirm
unto the said Christopher Marshall, Nathaniel Brown, Isaac
Howell, Peter Thomson, Moses Bartram, Jonathan Scholfield,
Benjamin Say, Joseph Warner, and Abraham Roberts, their
heirs and assigns, a certain lot or piece of ground (being the
northernmost part of the said described lot or piece of ground)
containing in breadth on the said Mulberry street forty-eight
feet, and in length or depth on the said Fifth street sixty feet,
bounded northward with the said Mulberry street, eastward
with the said Fifth street, southward with the remainder of
the above-described lot whereof this is part, and westward
with ground formerly of William Hudson, and now or late of

Joseph Wharton and Hannah his wife. Together also with
all and singular the building improvements, ways, waters,
water-courses, rights, liberties, privileges, hereditaments, and
appurtenances whatsoever thereunto belonging or in anywise
appertaining, and the reversions, remainders, rents, issues,
and profits thereof, and also all the estate, right, title, interest,
possession, property, claim and demand whatsoever of him,
the said Samuel Wetherill and Sarah his wife, in law, equity,
or otherwise howsoever, of, in, to, and out of the hereby
granted premises and every part thereof. To Have and to
Hold the said described lot or piece of ground, forty-eight
feet in breadth by sixty feet in length, hereditaments and
premises hereby granted, bargained, and sold or mentioned
so to be, with the appurtenances unto the said Christopher
Marshall, Nathaniel Brown, Isaac Howell, Peter Thomson,
Moses Bartram, Jonathan Scholfield, Benjamin Say, Joseph
Warner, and Abraham Roberts, and the survivors and survivor of them, and the heirs and assigns of such survivor forever. In Trust to and for the uses and purposes hereinafter
mentioned, limited, and declared, and to and for no other
use, intent, or purpose whatsoever; that is to say, to and for
the use and benefit of the Religious Society of People distinguished and known by the name of Free Quakers in the city
of Philadelphia, to erect and build a meeting house thereon,
and therein to meet for the solemn worship of Almighty God,
the Creator, Upholder and Ruler of the universe, and upon
this special trust and further confidence nevertheless, that
they, the said Christopher Marshall, Nathaniel Brown, Isaac
Howell, Peter Thomson, Moses Bartram, Jonathan Scholfield,
Benjamin Say, Joseph Warren, and Abraham Roberts, and
the survivors or survivor of them, or the heirs or assigns of
such survivor shall and will, from time to time, and as often

as need be or occasion require, by some good conveyance or assurance in the law, for the consideration of ten shillings grant, bargain, sell, release, and confirm the hereby granted premises, and every part thereof, to any number of persons, to be nominated by the said Religious Society, and the survivors and survivor of them, and the heirs and assigns of such survivor forever, In Trust for the uses and purposes aforesaid, and to and for no other use, intent, or purpose whatsoever, in order to maintain and support the contingent uses from being defeated or destroyed, and to make entries for the same, if it shall be needful, free and clear, and freely and clearly acquitted, exonerated, and discharged of and from the payment of the said yearly rent-charge of four pounds eight shillings, and every part thereof, and the said Samuel Wetherill, for himself, his heirs, executors, and administrators, doth covenant, promise, grant, and agree to and with the said Christopher Marshall, Nathaniel Brown, Isaac Howell, Peter Thomson, Moses Bartram, Jonathan Scholfield, Benjamin Say, Joseph Warner, and Abraham Roberts, their heirs and assigns, by these presents, in manner and form following; that is to say, that he, the said Samuel Wetherill, and his heirs the said described lot or piece of ground, hereditaments and premises hereby granted, bargained, and sold, or mentioned or intended so to be, with the appurtenances, unto the said Christopher Marshall, Nathaniel Brown, Isaac Howell, Peter Thomson, Moses Bartram, Jonathan Scholfield, Benjamin Say, Joseph Warner, and Abraham Roberts, their heirs and assigns, In Trust for the uses aforesaid against him the said Samuel Wetherill and his heirs, and against all and every other person or persons whatsoever lawfully claiming or to claim by, from, or under him, them, or any of them, shall and will warrant and forever defend by these presents; and

further, that he the said Samuel Wetherill, his heirs, or assigns, shall and will forever hereafter charge the remainder of
the said just described lot of ground, being forty feet in
breadth on the said Fifth street by forty-eight feet in depth,
with the payment of the said yearly rent-charge of four
pounds, eight shillings, and every part thereof, so as the same
rent shall not be extended or charged upon that part of the
said first described lot of ground hereby granted in trust for
the uses aforesaid, and of, and from the same yearly rent, and
of and from all actions, suits, distress and distresses, costs,
charges, damages, and demands whatsoever, shall and will
from time to time, and at all times hereafter, save, acquit,
defend, keep harmless, and indemnify the said Christopher
Marshall, Nathaniel Brown, Isaac Howell, Peter Thomson,
Moses Bartram, Jonathan Scholfield, Benjamin Say, Joseph
Warner, and Abraham Roberts, and the survivors and
survivor of them, and the heirs and assigns of such survivor of them and all their and every of their lands and
tenements, goods and chattels, and more especially the lot of
ground hereby granted with the buildings and improvements
thereon erected or to be erected ; and lastly, that he the said
Samuel Wetherill and his heirs, and all and every other person
or persons whatsoever, anything having or lawfully claiming,
or that shall or may so have or claim any estate, right, title,
or interest of, in, or to the said premises hereby granted or
mentioned to be granted, or of, in, or to any part or parcel
thereof, shall and will from time to time, and at all times
hereafter, upon the reasonable request and at the proper costs
and charges in the law of the said Christopher Marshall, Nathaniel Brown, Isaac Howell, Peter Thomson, Moses Bartram,
Jonathan Scholfield, Benjamin Say, Joseph Warner, and Abraham Roberts, their heirs and assigns, or some of them, make,

do, execute, and acknowledge or cause so to be, all and every such further and other reasonable act and acts, deed and deeds, conveyances and assurances in the law whatsoever, for the better and more perfect assurance and confirmation of the said described lot or piece of ground, hereditaments and premises hereby granted or mentioned or intended so to be, with the appurtenances, unto the said Christopher Marshall, Nathaniel Brown, Isaac Howell, Peter Thomson, Moses Bartram, Jonathan Scholfield, Benjamin Say, Joseph Warner, and Abraham Roberts, and the survivor and survivors of them, and the heirs and assigns of such survivor forever, in trust, for the uses aforesaid, and to and for no other use, intent, or purpose whatsoever, as by their or either of their Counsel learned in the law shall be reasonably devised, advised, or required.

In witness whereof, the said parties have interchangeably set their hands and seals hereunto, dated the day and year first above written.

Sealed and delivered in
   the presence of us
                          SAM'L. WETHERILL, JR., [SEAL]
  JONATHAN BARTOLETTE,   SARAH WETHERILL.   [SEAL]
  WILLIAM PERKINS,
  TY. MATLACK,

The tenth day of July, Anno Domini 1783, before me, Plunket Fleeson, Esquire, one of the justices, &c, for the city and county of Philadelphia, came the within named Samuel Wetherill and Sarah his wife, and acknowledged the within written indenture to be their act and deed, and desired the same may be recorded as such according to law. The said Sarah thereunto voluntarily consenting, she being of full age, separate and apart from her husband by me

91

examined, and the contents thereof first made known unto her.

Witness my hand and seal, the day and year aforesaid.

PLUNKET FLEESON, [SEAL]

Recorded in the office for recording deeds, &c., for the city and county of Philadelphia, in Deed Book D No. 7, page 193, July 16th, 1783.

Notes of Deeds to Trustees—Conveying the Real Estate held in Trust for the Religious Society of Free Quakers.

Deed.—Moses Bartram, Jonathan Scholfield, and Benjamin Say, Surviving Trustees to Samuel Wetherill Jr., George Kemble, Anthony Ruston, Joshua Lippincott, Thomas Say, Samuel Yorke, and John Wetherill—Trustees—dated August 13, 1808, recorded February 27, 1810, in Deed Book I. C. No 6, page 215 &c.

Deed.—Benjamin Say, sole surviving Trustee to same— dated same day, recorded September 9th, 1808, in Deed Book E. F. No. 30, page 565 &c.

Deed.—Joshua Lippincott surviving Trustee to John Price Wetherill, Edward Wetherill, George D. Wetherill, John P. Wetherill Jr., Charles Kemble, Joshua Lippincott Jr., and Samuel W. Lippincott—Trustees—dated April 18, 1853, recorded April 19, 1853, in Deed Book T. H. No. 74, page 344 &c.

Deed (endorsed on above).—Edward Wetherill, George D. Wetherill, John P. Wetherill (late Jr.), Charles Kemble, Joshua Lippincott (late Jr.), and Samuel W. Lippincott, Surviving Trustees to William Wetherill, John P. Wetherill, Samuel W. Lippincott, William Lippincott, Samuel Wetherill, Edward Wetherill, George D. Wetherill, Charles Kemble, and Henry M. Wetherill—Trustees—dated November 29th 1856, recorded June 13, 1882, in Deed Book J. O'D. No. 45, page 186, &c.

Deed.—John P. Wetherill, William Lippincott, Samuel Wetherill Jr., Edward Wetherill, and Henry M. Wetherill, Surviving Trustees to John P. Wetherill, William Lippincott Samuel Wetherill Sr., Edward Wetherill, Henry M. Wetherill, William Henry Wetherill, Christopher Wetherill Jr., Charles Wetherill, and Albert Lawrence Wetherill, Trustees—dated April 13, 1882, recorded June 13, 1882, in Deed Book J. O'D No. 45, page 181, &c.

Of the above Trustees Samuel Wetherill Sr., John P. Wetherill, and William Lippincott, are since deceased and Edward Wetherill has resigned.

Appendix No. 9.

Copy of " An Act for vesting certain City Lots therein
mentioned in trustees for a burial ground for the
use of the Religious Society of Free Quakers
in the City of Philadelphia," passed 26th
of August, 1786.

Private act Recorded in Law Book, No. III, p. 121.

Whereas the Religious Society of Friends called Free Quakers
in the city of Philadelphia, presented a petition to this House,
setting forth that the said Society hath been established by those
who were disowned by the people called Quakers, on account
of their attachment to the cause of their country, during the
great and important conflict for freedom and independence,
and have thereby been deprived of their religious rights and
privileges in that society, without even a distant probability
of a reunion with them upon consistent principles. That the
said Society of Free Quakers thus established through necessity arising out of a great revolution, had with the assistance
of their Christian fellow citizens purchased a lot of ground
and erected thereon a Meeting House of their own to perform worship in to Almighty God, which having thus accomplished, they nevertheless find themselves at a loss for a
place to bury their dead, and therefore prays the house for a
grant for a suitable lot of land for this religious and benevolent purpose. AND WHEREAS *it is but right and just to forward
the designs of religion and benevolence, and that the virtuous*

93

citizens of this Commonwealth who have been deprived of their religious rights and privileges on account of their attachment to the cause of their country in the time of its utmost danger, should have the encouragement of the Legislature. Therefore, be it enacted, and it is hereby enacted by the Representatives of the Freemen of the Commonwealth of Pennsylvania in General Assembly met, and by the authority of the same : —

That Eight of the City Lots belonging to the Commonwealth marked in the plan or draft of the public city lots. Nos. 34, 35, 36, 37, 38, 39, 40, 41, situate contiguous to each other on the West side of the Fifth Street from Delaware River in the city of Philadelphia, containing altogether in breadth North and South on the said Fifth Street One hundred and seventy six feet (that is to say Twenty two feet each lot) and in length or depth East and West, One hundred and ninety eight feet, six inches, bounded Northward by lot No. 42 sold to John Taylor, Eastward by Fifth Street aforesaid, and Westward by the back ends of Sixth Street lots, with their appurtenances shall be and hereby are vested in Christopher Marshall, Joseph Stiles, Nathaniel Brown, Isaac Howell, Peter Thompson, Benjamin Say and Joseph Warner (members of said religious society) and the survivors and survivor of them, and the heirs and assigns of such survivor, forever. In Trust, nevertheless, to and for the sole purpose of a burial ground for the use of the Religious Society of Friends distinguished and known by the name of Free Quakers in the City of Philadelphia, and to and for no other use, trust, intent or purpose whatever.

Appendix No. 10.

Copy of Entry on the First and Second pages of the
Book of Members of the Free Quakers, which
members of meeting sign, or in which their
names are entered by their parents.

The great end for which it pleaseth the Almighty to bring
Mankind into Existence, is, that they may faithfully serve him
here on Earth, and glorify him forever hereafter. He in his
infinite Goodness is constantly calling upon them to come
and learn of him, who is Wisdom itself: and we doubt not,
but that those who adhere to his divine Instructions will be
rewarded with Everlasting Peace, and for his manifold Mercies
bestowed upon us, believe it to be our Duty, publickly to
assemble together, to offer to him our grateful Acknowledge-
ments and tribute of Divine Worship. We do therefore unite
ourselves together as Members of this Religious Society called
by some the "Free Quakers": a Society established upon
enlarged and benevolent principles of the Gospel and hope to
profess true Christian Charity and that Divine Love which
enlargeth the Heart towards all Men and leadeth to hope and
believe, that however divided the Church militant may be, on
Earth, that yet the Church triumphant in Heaven is made up
of all Nations, Kindreds, Tongues and People, who with the
Harps of God in their hands are praising him on Mount Zion.

We think it proper to add, as we have heretofore declared
in an Address published in the early Institution of this

Society, "that we have no design to form Creeds or Confessions of Faith, but humbly to confide in those sacred Lessons of Wisdom and Benevolence which have been left us by Christ and his Apostles, contained in the Holy Scriptures and appealing to that Divine principle breathed by the Breath of God into the Hearts of all Men, to leave every Man to think and judge for himself according to the abilities received, and to answer for his Faith and opinion to him who seeth the Secrets of all Hearts, the sole Judge and sovereign Lord of Conscience.''

Being now through divine Favor in some measure established as a religious Society, we trust by an adherence to those Catholic Principles, we shall be favoured with the Blessing of the Almighty, and therefore relying on him for Protection, we do hereunto subscribe our Names and the names of our children, as Brethren and Sisters in Community, the seventeenth day of the Second Month, called February, in the year of our Lord, One Thousand seven hundred and eighty-five.

Appendix No. 11.

LETTER FROM SAMUEL WETHERILL.

To the Second Day's Morning Meeting of Ministers and Elders, of the People Called Quakers in the City of Philadelphia :—

I have received a verbal message by Henry Drinker which I understood came from you : On this message I propose to make a few remarks. Such are the effects of long established forms in society, that I have no reason to expect I shall convince you of the impropriety of your message ; yet I request you will read what I have to offer with as much candour as you can command on the occasion : I shall then be perfectly easy at whatever conclusions you may draw, or conduct you may observe towards me in the future part of your lives.

The message delivered to me was to the following purport, and as nearly verbatim as my memory serves me : Viz. "Thou must remember what is written 'When thou comest "to offer thy gift if thou rememberest that thy Brother hath "ought against thee, first go and be reconciled to thy Bro- "ther, and then come and offer thy gift : ' Thy appearing as "thou hast done has given pain to friends ; we wish thee to "be quiet in future ; for a person appearing on such occasions, "making the appearance of a friend, and one we have no "unity with ; is what friends cannot dispense with, we there- "fore wish thee to be quiet in future ; but if thou shouldst

7   97

"not, friends will be under the necessity of declaring pub-
"licly, that thou art not in fellowship with them."

Before I reply to the foregoing, permit me a little to pre-
mise. The subject is serious. It is now many years since the
Lord in a way not less than miraculous, visited my soul with
his Love and Light, giving me to see a Beauty in a virtuous
life far greater than any one can comprehend who has not
had the same Divine prospect; for altho' most men will admit the necessity of virtue, yet no man living sees fully into
its beauty and infinite importance, until the Divine Light in
an extraordinary manner opens it to him. This prospect
ravished my soul, and begot in me so ardent a Love to the
Lord, as that I then knew, and felt, what it was that supported the Martyrs in the flames; for I thought, if I had then
an hundred lives, I could have sacrificed them all, if it had
been required, for the Testimony of Jesus. At this time I
entered into covenant with my God, and made a total conse-
cration of my heart to him. This was the day of my espou-
sal to the beloved of Souls. This experience thus related is
not meant to make a parade of superiour virtue. I am far
from feeling any vanity of this kind, I know my weaknesses
and confess them, am poor, and have often stumbled in the
way cast up for the redeemed to walk in; and have much
reason to be concerned that so Divine a favour together with
many others since, have not produced a greater effect: But
from the day of my first visitation untill the present day, I
have thought it my duty, by example and sometimes by precept, to recommend to Mankind those things on which their
present and future felicity depends. That this has been done
but in an imperfect manner is confessed.

I now proceed to remark upon your message as delivered
by Henry Drinker, viz: That before I offered my gift I

should first be reconciled to my Brother. It is not necessary for me to explain what I conceive to be the meaning of this text as delivered by our Lord. I expect you mean by it, that I should first be restored to fellowship with you, before I attempted to persuade any person to be serious, and prepare for death, and that it is an exceeding great offence if done upon a spot of ground in which you claim a propriety. Supposing myself, or any other person among the least of Mankind, on so serious an occasion as that of a fellow creature being suddenly summoned into the immediate presence of the great Judge of Heaven and Earth, should feel a fervent wish that all might be prepared when the summons should be sent to them. In such a case would it be absolutely necessary to suspend expressing this wish until the person was admitted into fellowship with you? If so, he then misses the opportunity and another may never happen. Men of all denominations are usually invited to attend the funeral of their fellow-citizens; Jews, Turks and Heathens might be present on such an occasion : Jews, Turks, and Heathens believe in a future existence and that the virtuous will be happy and the wicked miserable. Now suppose the mind of either such person to be deeply impressed on an occasion so serious, and that either Turk, Jew or Heathen should exhort every one present to be serious and endeavour to prepare for Death, I ask you my Brethren what possible ground could there be in such case for offence? All who are invited to attend on those occasions are on an equality: Death is common to all men; every one is alike interested in the awfull consequences, and therefore none can have exclusive privileges to give advice on those occasions. When the Lord represents to the mind the absolute necessity of preparation for Death, all have an equal right in his fear to express their wish for their fellow creatures, or to exhort them to prepare for this awful change; and that any one person whatever, making a profession of Piety should be offended at it is strange. I expect you admit that it is every man's duty to wish well for his neighbor. And, if so, then every man has a right and ought to be at liberty to do good to his neighbour, either by his advice or in such way as he may think most proper, so that a real good be the object: to the Lord alone is he accountable for the way and manner. This is not intended to vindicate an intrusion either upon you, or upon any other persons. For as every Man has a right to give his advice on any important occasion, he being accountable to the Lord, so every other Man has a right also either to receive or to reject as he pleases what is so offered, he or they being accountable only to the Lord: so that you as individuals or as a body, have a right to receive or reject, any advice which may be offered to you by any person whatever. But where there is a promiscuous multitude of all persuasions collected together on an occasion interesting to all, there your publickly opposing what might be offered, would render you highly to blame; for there are numbers not under the same prejudices with you, and what you would reject, might be suited to the conditions of others, and well received by them. You may say, as Henry Drinker said; we have a rule to the contrary. It may be so, but you ought not to have such a rule. It is an infringement upon the rights of all Men, and not only so, but you presumptuously infringe upon the prerogative of the Lord, you thereby attempt to circumscribe his grace, and limit his Divine Light upon the human soul. You may object again and say, If persons have a right to come into our Graveyards and give us advice, they have the same right to come into our Meeting Houses, and impose their advice upon us there. To this I reply, the cases are not similar. That freedom which a person might use innocently, or what might be the duty of him to express whose mind was seriously impressed at a funeral to a promiscuous multitude, might yet be very improper if exercised when you were assembled in your places for worship. There is a Divine reason and fitness in things which the upright see into and which cannot be determined or prescribed by any litteral rule. A Man, not of your society, would be either right or wrong in speaking among you, according as he was either especially qualified or not, and the strong prejudices which you have against other Societies, altho it be your fault, it yet ought to make every person exceedingly cautious, and examine well his authority, if he supposed it his duty, in your places of Worship to give you advice ; for all should take care if possible not to offend those who even labor under the most deep-rooted prejudices. Now altho' every Man who might apprehend it his duty to give you advice should be extremely careful not to offend you if possible, and it is granted that you have a right either to hear him, or to refuse to hear him, you being accountable only to the Lord for your exercising this right ; yet my brethren on this subject I will give you my opinion even tho' it will have no weight. It is safest to hear what any sober man may have to say on the all important subject of Piety and virtue : this will give you no pain in a dying hour; the opposing him might. You should not forget the error of Judgment the Apostles of our Lord were under ; for altho' they were immediately commissioned by him to preach the Gospel, and to work Miracles in his name, yet such was their weakness that they forbad others doing the same, because they followed not with them ; but remember they were not justified for this, but reproved by their Master.

Friends should also remember the liberty which their forefathers took in going into the places of Worship of other Societies and speaking among them, and in their burying grounds down to the present day. To this you will say; It was their duty to do so; But it cannot be the duty of a person of another Society to come and Preach to friends. The vanity of this declaration is exceeding great. If it is improper for a person not of your Society to give an exhortation at a funeral among you, or in your place of Worship, upon what principle is it right in you to exhort at the funerals of others, and in the place of Worship of other Societies? Are you as a Society quite compleat in all Christian Graces, and have you all divine qualifications bestowed upon you exclusively to the rest of Men, so as that it is impossible to suppose the Lord could with any propriety authorize any other person beside a Quaker to speak to you? Can you shew that you have an exclusive right to that divine illumination which expands the heart, and warms it with good will towards all men? Untill you can shew that every member among you is so perfect as that friendly advice bestowed upon them is altogether needless, or that qualification to give advice is possessed by you exclusively, your forbidding any person to give advice anywhere is improper. It is indeed, as has been observed, presuming to limit the Authority of the Highest, and is an attempt to prevent the Salvation of Men. But do not my friends suppose from this, that I have any inclination to visit you in this way. I hope that no such thing will ever happen; it would be the most painful task ever required of me, so unwilling am I to offend you, or to have any altercation with you.

Having remarked as above, it may not be improper to shew you, that whilst you are faulting persons and proceeding against them in a high tone of unwarranted authority, for simply offering advice to such as are willing to receive it, without meaning an offence, or an obtrusion upon any; you are at the same time indecently intruding with your advice upon the clear and unquestionable rights of others. I could illustrate this by a variety of instances, but for brevity sake one shall suffice. I consider the Monthly Meeting and the select meeting of Philadelphia, as one body. Some friends by deputation from the monthly meeting waited upon two of my sons to deal with them for joining another religious Society. I was present at the conversation and the friends were treated with great decency and had a clear and full answer given them by my sons, that they chose to go to the same place of worship with their father: A visit was notwithstanding afterwards repeated, at which I happened accidentally to be present, and as it was in my own House, and the business with my own children in whose welfare I am deeply interested, so I thought, I might without any impropriety say something on the occasion and more especially on such an occasion. What was said, was very civilly said. I was however replied to precisely to the following effect: That friends' business was with my children, and not with me, that I had no business there, and must have come to interrupt friends in their visit. That my children were of age and should judge for themselves, that their father was a prejudiced person and his advice not to be regarded.

If it be an intrusion of an aggravated kind for a person not of your Society to walk into your burying ground to attend a funeral and there to express a wish that all might be serious and prepare to die, how much greater is that intrusion you are guilty of, when after you had been decently received in my house, and a clear and full answer given you to your advice, you still repeat it, and claim a right, and exercise it too, to give your advice again and again, and tell myself I had no

business there, that my children should take your advice, and
not their Father's, for his they ought not to regard. Let me
ask you my friends—How would you treat men who should
act in the same way towards you, and your children? You
would I doubt not, expatiate upon such intrusion, and would
treat such persons with contempt. If there has been an impropriety in me in obtruding advice (which will be impossible
for you to prove) yet when compared with yours it is small,
and what our Lord said to a people formerly, who was apt to
find fault is applicable to you. "Why beholdest thou the
"mote that is in thy brother's eye, and seest not the beam
"which is in thine own: first take the beam out of thine
"own eye and then shalt thou see clearly how to take out
"the mote which is in thy Brother's eye."

Having made the foregoing observations on the rights of
Men, it remains to say a few words respecting another part of
your message. The writer of this has not an high opinion of
his gifts or abilities to promote the cause of virtue, he can
say however he wishes well to it sincerely, and in his feeble
engagements therein, sometimes feels a peace Men can neither
give nor take away. But yet he will confess to you, altho'
you have no authority to call him to an account, nor interfere
in his business, he at times feels some pain least he should
not have advanced so great and good a cause. But friends,
have there not been appearances among you which have given
you pain when the fault lay with yourselves? I was a diligent
attender of your meetings for near thirty years, and knew
that a part of your meeting were uneasy at the publick appearances of some whose Ministry they at length approved.
I well remember George Dillwyn's first appearance in the Ministry, and the opposition he met with. There was at that
time a particular intimacy between that friend and myself,

and as brethren we freely unbosomed our hearts to each other. After repeated opposition to him both in publick and private from members of your meeting, a committee told him plainly that they had not unity with his appearance : And they enjoined him not to break silence but to bear his burden, and more especially not to appear in Prayer, for if he did, they told him they would manifest their Testimony against him publickly by not joining with him, and in order still the more effectually to stop his mouth, one publick friend who is not now among the living, but who was in his day of distinguished note among you, wrote a letter to George, and in clear and express words told him, that he had neither part nor lot in the ministry, or, says the friend, "the Lord never spoke by me." As I knew the opposition to George arose from prejudice, and having a great love for him, I related to my Father-in-law what was carrying on against George, upon which my father appeared much surprised and altho' he was a member of your meeting, did not seem aware of what was doing ; which shews there may not always be unanimity among yourselves on business of this kind : for my Father immediately interested himself in George's favour and spoke to John Smith at Burlington (George having then removed there) and requested John to use his influence in George's favour, and I well knew that Mordecai Yarnal, Anthony Beneset and John Smith together with some other friends, whose names I could mention who were then members of your meeting, most of whom are since dead, so interposed in George's behalf that at length he was admitted a minister among you.

Upon the whole then, If the most eminent ministers among you at times give you pain, and you do with so much determination oppose men of your own Society, meerly upon ill founded prejudices, what must such poor creatures expect,

who have been declared by you not worthy of Christian fellowship. Is it possible after such a declaration, that you can
possess that simplicity and candour towards them in which
alone there is true discernment?

Further I was informed that if I should again appear as I
had done, friends would be under the necessity of informing
such who might be present that I was not in Unity with
friends.

If you entertain an Idea that I wish to avail myself of any
reputation which might result from a supposed membership
with you, you are under a great mistake. It has happened
divers times since I have been disowned, that I have fallen
in company with persons who had an esteem for friends, and
have found some respect paid me upon a supposition that I
belonged to the Society. Now it ever appeared to me a kind
of hypocrisy if I should let a person go away under such a
mistake, and enjoy that sort of reputation which I was not
entitled to, and have always undeceived them, frankly telling
them I was disowned by you: so that if such a case should
happen as you allude to, you have not only a right to do as
you say, but you have my entire approbation so to do; however in this explanation of yourselves, you ought to take care
not to defame me, there might be some persons present on
such an occasion, who might not be acquainted with the merits
of the case for which I was disowned ; such might suppose I
was disowned by you for some great immorality : be pleased
therefore to state the whole case, and I have neither right nor
inclination to prevent it, for I have scarcely ever met with
one person, either a member of your Society, or of any other,
who did not think I was hardly dealt with by you, and by far
the greater number consider you as the aggressor. A man
may be disowned by you, and held up as a spectacle of con-

tempt, who nevertheless may be owned by Christ at the day of general judgment, and admitted into fellowship with the Saints. But let us now enquire into the nature of that offence which was esteemed of such magnitude as to render it necessary to testify against me. It was simply for submitting to the dispensations of Divine Providence, which you yourselves have since done, for this no offence, have I been, and am still to be, held up by you in an odious light, and pains taken to stamp a prejudice against me upon the minds of the rising generation, so that when both you and I are dead and all of us in that most awfull state of existence, future generations may treat my memory as you have done my person. The amazing prejudices you labour under, and your conduct governed by those prejudices, operate as an injury for ages: And yet my friends you changed your sentiments with respect to the offence for which you disowned me, for you desisted from the business you begun, and many continued members of your meeting who yet acted as myself had done: And Anthony Beneset freely acknowledged to me you were wrong. The candour of this worthy Man in making this voluntary confession to one who before he had blamed, very much endeared him to me, it was a concession I neither expected nor sought for: But you, my friends not possessing his virtues, still persecute the Man whom you at first injured.

There are divers members of your meeting for whom I have always entertained an high esteem. I have taken them to be Persons of more enlarged and liberal minds than to act towards me as you do, were they not under the necessity of joining with you for form sake. If there are such among you, they are excepted in the censure comprehended in this address. But I may be mistaken, you may be unanimous, and it is possible your conduct may not be so much the effect of ill will towards me, as an error in your judgment, you have been accustomed to certain rules, perhaps long established, which you conceive indispensably necessary to observe ; how far this will excuse you at the day that is hastening is not for me to say ; but this dry, formal, undistinguishing sort of business, leads at times to the same conduct as that of the Scribes and Pharisees, who bid the Apostles be silent, and excommunicated Men for believing in Christ.

Altho' the writer of this is of little consequence in your esteem, nor of much in his own, he is yet serious in this address and thinks it is not inconsistent with a becoming degree of modesty to request you would read it with solid attention in your meeting ; tho' this he does not expect. But were you to do so, divested of prejudice, you might derive from it some instruction which would be of future service to you, both in your individual capacities, and as members of a Religious Society.

The foregoing was written just before the breaking out of the malignant fever, and was intended to have been sent to you then, but the writer's attention was taken off from this, on account of the extreem attention to his business which he was hurryed into, occasioned by the afforesaid disease, and the great mortality which hapened in consequence. The mentioning of which circumstance brings to his memory, the particulars of that exhortation which gave you offence, and occasioned your message to him. The writer does not pretend to the knowledge of future events, except those which must happen in the nature of things ; but Divine providence may make use of an instrument to give warning to prepare for those things which he may intend to bring about, without revealing to such instrument his particular designs. The writer well remembers his mind was seriously

impressed with the extreem shortness of our existence here;
and of the uncertainty of all things below; and of the infinite importance of a preparation for death; this prospect so
impressed his mind that he thought they were as powerfull
reasons for deep consideration and preparation for death, as if
the Lord should again at that instant commission an Angel to
declare, in the Awfull manner one formerly did to John the
Divine that time should be no longer. This prospect the writer
thought it his duty to express, and which he did as well as he
was then abilitated to do. And, my friends, let me ask you
what authority have you to reprove him for it? Has not the
great mortality with which the City has been visited, shewn
the propriety of such an exhortation from some person?
And how came you by a right to dictate either who should or
who should not be the instrument to urge those things. What
was then offered did not offend all who were present, I have
been assured, but on the contrary was well received; and the
late visitation esteemed a corroborating circumstance to shew
its propriety. Many who were then present are now no more
in mutability, and among this number is one, or more, of your
Meeting, and if the Ancient friend who probably reported
to you what happened, and no doubt agreed to the measure
adopted by you, had taken the advice then given, instead of
spurning at it, and so improved the few moments alloted to
him in the evening of his day, as was then sincerely urged,
it would have been acting a wiser part; and altho' we may
hope he is at rest, together with other members of your
meeting, who agreed in your message to the subscriber, yet
their officiousness in this business is now no cause or part of
their felicity, nor will it contribute to yours, my brethren, in
the day that is hastening. Your conduct towards the sub-

scriber, will not be among the good works in which the righteous rejoice.

Such is the esteem which the writer has entertained for divers members of your meeting, and so great has been his desire to live upon the most friendly terms with them, that he is sorry he is obliged to write as he has done ; he wishes sincerely to cultivate the most cordial friendship for his fellow Christians of all denominations ; he therefore hopes there are divers members of your meeting to whom the censure contained in this address is not applicable, it would give him pain to think otherwise, because he wishes still to love and esteem them. But if your meeting is unanimous and those persons so loved and esteemed look upon the subscriber in that point of view which the meeting's conduct towards him fully implies, he will endeavor to bear with their prejudices and patiently wait the event of all things here below, hoping and believing his weak efforts to promote the cause of virtue, will through his Master's clemency finally receive his approbation. And being supported in this faith and confidence he hopes when Jesus commissions, he shall undismayed at all fit times and places warn Men to prepare for an Awfull Eternity. Your advice and threats are therefore my friends, considered in the same light, as if you forbid the writer, to Love his Lord and Saviour.

SAML. WETHERILL.

PHILADELPHIA, *11mo. 23rd, 1793.*

Appendix No. 12.

LIST OF MEMBERS

OF THE

FREE QUAKER SOCIETY

Who are Known or Believed to be Deceased.

Isaac Howell, Trustee, 1783.
Robert Parrish.
James Sloane.
White Matlack, Treasurer, 1784.
Moses Bartram, Trustee, 1783.
Benjamin Say, Trustee, 1783.
Samuel Wetherill, Clerk, Feb. 20, 1781, to Sept. 1, 1808.
Owen Biddle.

The above attended the first meeting of the Society, February 20, 1781.

Nathaniel Allen, ... 1781	Abner Buckman, ... 1782
Matthew Ash, ... 1781	John Buckman, Jr., ... 1782
Jonathan Ash, ... 1781	Nathaniel Browne, ... 1781
	Trustee, ... 1783
	Clement Biddle, ... 1781
John Bartram, ... 1781	Thomas Bryan, ... 1781
James Bartram, ... 1781	Joseph Burden, ... 1785
John Bell, ... 1782	Margaret Boggs, ... 1785
James Boone, ... 1782	Margaret Boggs, ... 1847
Joseph Bonsall, ... 1781	Timothy (son of Guy) Bryan, 1847
Joshua Bonsall, ... 1781	William P. Bryan, ... 1832
Jonathan Bonsall, ... 1781	Martha Bryan, ... 1810
Enoch Betts, ... 1782	Peter Barker, ... 1781

Samuel Crispin, ... 1785	Susanna Elton (Jr.), ... 1785
William Crispin, ... 1781	John Elton, ... 1785
Thomas Crispin, ... 1781	Thomas Elton (Jr.), ... 1785
Lydia Crispin, ... 1785	Elizabeth Elton, ... 1785
Lydia Crispin, Jr., ... 1785	Anthony Elton, ... 1785
Samuel Crispin, Jr., ... 1785	Samuel Eldridge, ... 1785
George Chandler, ... 1781	
Thomas Coats, ... 1781	William Fisher [(Jr.), ... 1781
John Claypoole, ... 1785	Samuel Foulke (of Richland), 1782
Elizabeth Claypoole, ... 1785	J. Fisher, ... 1781
Martha Coats, ... 1785	
Sarah Coats, ... 1785	Nathaniel Gibson, ... 1781
John Chapman, ... 1782	Rebecca W. Gumbes, . . . 1789
Samuel Crawford, ... 1786	Samuel W. Gumbes, ... 1830
Elizabeth Crawford, ... 1786	Joseph Govett, ... 1781
Mary Crawford, ... 1786	Edward Griffiths, ... 1785
Charles Crawford, ... 1786	
Elizabeth Crawford (Jr.), . . 1786	Caleb Hewes, ... 1781
Sarah Cribs, ... 1786	Henry Hayes, ... 1781
Mary Crips, ... 1785	Samuel Howell, ... 1781
Hannah Carmalt, ... 1785	Edward Heston, ... 1781
Isaac Collins (of Trenton), . 1781	Isaac Heston, ... 1782
Elizabeth Champion, ... 1847	Clara Hanna, ... 1847
	Thomas Hopkins, ... 1781
William Darragh, ... 1781	Sarah W. Hough, ... 1845
Lydia Darragh, ... 1781	Frances E. A. E. Hough, . 1874
Ann Darragh, ... 1781	Sophia Hildebron, ... 1847
Susanna Darragh, ... 1781	
James Delaplaine, ... 1781	Robert Jones, ... 1781
Cadwalader Dickinson, . . . 1781	Maria L. Janeway, ... 1830
Jonathan Draper, ... 1782	
Thomas Dyer, ... 1782	Jacob Karcher, ... 1785
Timothy Davis, ... 1782	Elinor Karcher, ... 1785
	Margaretta Karcher, ... 1785
Jehu Eldridge, ... 1781	George Kemble, ... 1805
Joshua Ely, ... 1782	Charles Kemble. 1820
Nathaniel Ellicot, ... 1782	Maria Kemble, ... 1832
Edward Evans, ... 1781	Samuel Kemble, ... 1832
Evan Evans, ... 1781	Johanna Kemble, ... 1832
David Evans, ... 1781	Emily Kemble, ... 1832
Thomas Elton, ... 1785	Charlotte H. Kemble, . . . 1832
Susanna Elton, ... 1785	Elizabeth F. Kemble, . . . 1832
Mary Elton, ... 1785	Joseph Kemble, ... 1832

8

Appendix, No. 13.

NAMES AND RESIDENCES OF THE PRESENT FREE QUAKERS, 1894.

Frances S. D. Gumbes,	1706 Pine St.
Isabel G. Cresson,	" "
Francis M. Cresson,	" "
Isabel Cresson,	" "
Caleb Cresson, Jr.,	" "
Susan V. Cresson,	" "
Georgine Cresson,	" "
Mary G. Barker,	425 South 16th St.
Elizabeth H. Barker,	" " "
George G. Barker,	" " "
Frances Gumbes, Jr.,	1706 Pine St.
Dr. Charles W. Gumbes,	Oaks, Pa.
Rebecca W. Gumbes,	" "
Charles W. Gumbes, Jr.,	" "
Francis Gumbes,	" "
S. Wetherill Gumbes,	" "
Jos. Hildeburn Gumbes,	" "
Mr. and Mrs. A. Lawrence Wetherill,	1100 Spruce St.
John Price Wetherill,	Bethlehem, Pa.
Ira Cortright Wetherill,	" "
Anna Wetherill,	" "
Florence Wetherill,	" "
John Price Wetherill, Jr.,	" "
William C. Wetherill,	" "
C. A. Hecksches Wetherill,	" "
Mr. and Mrs. Samuel P. Wetherill,	Edgewater Park, N. J
Samuel P. Wetherill, Jr.,	" " "
Georgine W. Smith,	" " "
Sarah Wetherill,	" " "
Christine N. Wetherill, 2d,	" " "
Isabel Wetherill,	" " "

William C. Wetherill, ...	Joplin, Mo.
Elizabeth C. Wetherill, ...	" "
Gertrude Wetherill, ...	" "
Mrs. Georgiana W. Cox, ...	Bethlehem, Pa.
Walter W. Cox, ...	" "
William John Cox, ...	" "
Sarah W. Cox, ...	" "
Eugenia Cox, ...	" "
Madeleine Cox, ...	" "
Mrs. Thyrza A. Wetherill, ...	421 School Lane, Germantown.
Elisha K. K. Wetherill, ...	" " " "
Maria K. Apperson, ...	" " " "
Jacob J. Janeway, ...	Greensburg, Pa.
Lawrence W. Janeway, ...	" "
Joseph B. Janeway, ...	" "
Mr. and Mrs. Price W. Janeway, . .	Media, Pa.
Price W. Janeway, Jr., ...	" "
Helen H. Janeway, ...	" "
Maria K. Janeway, ...	2316 Locust St.
Dr. and Mrs. Herman Burgin, . . .	72 W. Chelten Ave., Germantown.
Mrs. Rachel W. J. Hodge, ...	2316 Locust St.
Mr. and Mrs. John L. Janeway, Jr.,	Phœnixville, Pa.
John L. Janeway, 3d, ...	" "
Augustin S. Janeway, ...	" "
Sibyl Kent Janeway, ...	" "
Mrs. Emily M. Foster, ...	1710 Pine St.
Mrs. Martha W. Brinckerhoff, ...	" " "
William A. Foster, ...	" " "
Elizabeth W. Douglass, ...	" " "
Mrs. Mary C. Wetherill, ...	La Fayette, Ind.
Mrs. Anna B. O'Ferrall, ...	" "
Dr. Richard B. Wetherill, ...	" "
Mr. and Mrs. Henry M. Wetherill, . .	15 East Penn St., Germantown.
Charles Wetherill, ...	" " " "
Dr. and Mrs. Henry M. Wetherill, Jr.,	2208 Locust St.
Mrs. Rebecca W. Tiers, ...	126 Pomona Terrace, Germantown.
Rebecca W. Tiers, Jr., ...	" " " "
Mary Tiers, ...	" " " "
Paul L. Tiers, ...	" " " "
Helen Tiers, ...	" " " "
Thomas M. Wetherill, ...	New Orleans, La.
Mrs. Julia W. Baker, ...	" "
Mrs. Margaretta M. Kernan, ...	" "

Clive N. Kernan, ... New Orleans, La.
Mayer Wetherill, ... Syracuse, N. Y.
Mrs. Margaretta M. Diehl, ... 2312 Spruce St.
Mrs. Margaretta W. Wallace, ... Staten Island, N. Y.
Mrs. Mary E. W. Smith, ... 1613 Spruce St.
Edward I. Smith, Jr., ... " " "
Mrs. Susan D. Edson, ... 2312 Spruce St.
Charles W. Diehl, ... " " "
William E. Diehl, ... " " "
Thomas J. Diehl, ... " " "
Samuel Wetherill, ... 1835 De Lancey Place.
Col. John M. Wetherill, ... Pottsville, Pa.
Mr. and Mrs. William H. Wetherill, . 37th and Walnut Sts.
H. Emerson Wetherill, ... " " " "
Herbert Wetherill, ... " " " "
Abel P. Wetherill, ... " " " "
Webster K. Wetherill, ... " " " "
Francis M. Wetherill, ... " " " "
Mrs. Rachel Hewson, ... 1434 Spruce St.
Isabel Hewson, ... " " "
Emily Hewson, ... " " "
Mrs. Mary H. Booraem,
Addinell Hewson, M. D., ... 1508 Pine St.
William K. Hewson,
Mr. and Mrs. Frank D. Wetherill, . . 1723 Pine St.
Isabel Wetherill, ... " " "
Brinton Wetherill, ... " " "
J. Lawrance Wetherill, ... " " "
Caroline B. Wetherill, ... " " "
Lt. Charles S. Riché, U. S. A.,
Capt. Alexander M. Wetherill, U. S. A.
Mrs. Agnes Dundas Lippincott, . . . 1333 Walnut St.
James Dundas Lippincott, ... 509 South Broad St.
J. Wurtz Dundas, ... 1333 Walnut St.
Benjamin W. Richards, ... 45 South 17th St.
Mrs. James Constable, ... 1820 DeLancey Place.
Miss Constable, ... " " "
Howard R. Constable, ... " " "
Stevenson Constable, ... " " "
Mrs. Augustus H. Richards, ... 4049 Locust St.
Mary Lippincott Richards, ... " " "
Alfred Wetherill, ... Elkton, Md.
Miss Jane Wetherill, ... 3915 Woodland Ave.

Miss Ellen Wetherill, ... 3915 Woodland Ave.
Miss Sarah Y. Wetherill, ... "   "   "
Mrs. W. W. Young, ... "   "   "
Miss Marion Yorke Young, ... "   "   "
Miss Ella Young, ... "   "   "
Miss Julia Young, ... "   "   "
Mr. and Mrs. Edward Wetherill, . . 1413 Spruce St.
Miss Edith Wetherill, ... "   "   "
Miss Marian Wetherill, ... "   "   "
Miss Blanche Wetherill, ... "   "   "
Miss Irma Wetherill, ... "   "   "
Miss Cora Wetherill, ... "   "   "
Miss Rebecca Wetherill, ... 1340 Walnut St.
Miss Ida Cushman, ... "   "   "
Miss Alice Cushman, ... "   "   "
Mrs. Susan M. Miller, ... 2036 Vine St.
Mrs. Anna Wetheriil, ... 325 South 16th St.
Mr. and Mrs George D. Wetherill, . "   "   "
Thomas Wetherill, ... "   "   "
Mr. and Mrs. Christopher Wetherill Jr., 5532 Morris St., Germantown.
Mrs. Percy Browne, ... Roxbury, Mass.
Miss Katharine W. Browne, ...   "
Percy Browne, Jr., ...   "
Mrs. George Northrop, ... Edgewater Park, N. J.,
Mrs. Isabel N. McHenry, ...   "   "
Dr. Katharine Northrop, ... 316 South 16th St.
Mrs. Morris Hacker, ... (In Europe).
Miss Beulah Hacker, ...   "
Mrs. Isabel H. Dixon. . . . . . . 58th St. near Elmwood Ave.
Charles C. Wetherill, ... Kingston, Md.
C. Whittington Wetherill, ...   "
Samuel Wetherill, Jr., ...   "
Edward Wetherill, ...   "
Alfred N. Wetherill, ... Strafford, Pa.
William S. Wetherill, ...   "
Morris H. Wetherill, ...   "
Mrs. A. T. Zeising, ... 2029 North 8th St.
Miss Zeising, ... "   "   "
Miss Anna Maria Kemble, ... "   "   "
Mrs. Sarah Kemble Eichler, ... "   "   "
Nicholas Helverson, ... "   "   "